They Left the Valley Behind

They Left the Valley Behind

The Boys of
Bacup & Rawtenstall Grammar School
Who Died in World War One

Anne King

Acknowledgments

I am indebted to many people and organisations for their help. A big thank you goes to Moira Cowie for her painstaking editing and helpful comments. The manuscript would not have reached the publication stage without her assistance. Thanks are also due to Bacup & Rawtenstall Grammar School for providing access to the information collated by the late Headmaster, Mr Philip Lane Clark, now held in the School's archives. The few discrepancies found in his work are completely understandable, since his research was carried out without the benefit of current online sources or the 1911 census data. I am particularly grateful to him for the Newchurch Grammar School admission information, which included details of feeder schools.

I would like to thank staff at the National Library in London and Boston Spa, Rossendale and Haslingden libraries and the Bacup Natural History Museum for the access to local newspaper archives. SM-MEN Syndication, and in particular the Regional Manager of Reach Syndication, Lawrence Matheson, answered my queries and gave permission for the use of items and photographs from the archives of the Bacup Chronicle, Bacup Times, Haslingden Guardian and Rossendale Free Press. The photographs of Ronald Andrew and Frank Mitchell are included with the permission of NatWest Group Archives under their "Reproduction of Archive and Art Material" Licence.

My grateful thanks must go to the independent researcher Simon Fowler, whose many journeys to the National Archives on my behalf enabled me to access records unavailable online. Members of the online Great War Forum answered every one of my endless questions, often within minutes of my posting the request. Never once did they question my limited knowledge of Corps and Divisional organisation, military tactics, weaponry or terminology. Their enthusiasm for their subject was an inspiration.

Particular mention should be made of the following museum archivists and curators who gave me access to regimental histories and diaries in their collections: Peter Donnelly, King's Own Royal Regiment Museum in Lancaster; Liam Hart, Museum of the Manchester Regiment, Ashton-under-Lyne; Philip Mather, Lancashire Fusiliers Museum, Bury; Thomas Mallinson, Lancashire Infantry Museum, Preston.

I have to thank my husband, who never complained about the many months of research I undertook or the mountains of files, books and papers I stored around the house. In particular, I have to thank him for all the driving he undertook on our many visits to the Somme & Flanders battlefields. With his help and patience, and better sense of direction, we visited and photographed the grave or memorial of every Newchurch Grammar School old boy who died on the Western Front. For those buried or remembered elsewhere, with the exception of two graves we visited in Rossendale, I have to thank The War Graves Photographic Project for their images. The website Rutland Remembers supplied the photograph of Cologne Cemetery and Hardman Lodge 1948 gave me permission to photograph their memorial to James Pinnington. Andrew Gill provided images from The Keasbury-Gordon Photograph Archive. Finally I must thank Francesca Bartalini Waudby for her beautiful cover design.

If there are inaccuracies in any of the personal or service details attributed to any of the men named in this account, I shall be happy to make amendments on receipt of relevant information. Please e-mail: AnneKKing1953@gmail.com

Table of Contents

Preface 1
Introduction 3
Chapter 1 7
    Edward Philips Jackson 8
    James Hutchinson 12
Chapter 2 16
    James Tomlinson 17
Chapter 3 21
    Alan Booth 24
Chapter 4 29
    Ernest Jackson 32
    Albert Aspden 36
    John Percy Turnbull 40
Chapter 5 45
    Tom Fielding 46
    Frank Hitchin 50
Chapter 6 54
    Wilfred Crowther 56
    Edward Martin Wright 60
    Fred Howorth 65
    John Elwyn Slater 69
Chapter 7 73
    Ronald Andrew 75
    Joseph Harvey 79

Chapter 8	83
Frank Horrocks	85
Lionel Norman Shepherd	88
Chapter 9	92
John Edward Winterbottom	96
Percy Horsfield	101
Albert Wray Titterington	106
Arthur Taylor	112
Chapter 10	117
Jessie Hargreaves Temperley	119
Vernon Radcliffe Stewart	125
James Arthur Ray	130
Chapter 11	135
Norman Wilkinson	139
Albert John Holt	144
Michael Heys	149
James Greenwood Collinge	155
Willie Rae Walker Pickup	160
Norman Whittaker	164
Sidney Worswick Ashworth	170
Frank Warley Mitchell	175
James Pinnington	181
Chapter 12	185
Harry Smith	187

Chapter 13 192
    Edward Hall Holden 195
    Richard Crawshaw Hardman 199
    Reginald Alfred Stock 203
Chapter 14 208
Appendix 209
Bibliography & Sources 211
Index 217

Author's Note

Each of the thirty-seven men on the Roll of Honour has been positively identified using a variety of sources currently available to researchers. Individual service records have proved invaluable, but a large number of these files were destroyed during the 1940 London Blitz. Where National Archives information is reproduced, it is with kind permission of HMSO under the Open Government Licence. Unfortunately, I have been unable to source a photograph for all the men on the Roll of Honour, and should like to hear from anyone who can provide copies of those that are missing.

Roll of Honour 1914-1918[1]

---

[1] Photograph by C R Scott - Bacup & Rawtenstall Grammar School

Preface

There are two memorial plaques in the entrance foyer of Bacup & Rawtenstall Grammar School in Rossendale, Lancashire. They remember old boys of the school who died in the two world wars. Many surnames are familiar to me, the same as those of pupils with whom I had contact during my years working at the school. Others are those of well-known families whose links to the Rossendale Valley stretch back over many decades.

Although the memorials are at BRGS, all but the youngest on the WW1 panel attended Newchurch Grammar School. This boys' school was founded on endowed land in the early eighteenth century and later moved to a new building in Newchurch. By the 1900s the school had become severely overcrowded and, with no room for expansion, a replacement was built in Waterfoot and opened in 1913. Renamed Bacup & Rawtenstall Secondary & Technical School, this was where the youngest man on the memorial was educated.[2] The 1913 building has been incorporated into the current BRGS site.

For many, the Roll of Honour may be no more than a list of names from a conflict fought over a century ago. The aim of this account is to discover more about the men behind the names and in doing so to acknowledge the sacrifice that each man made while serving King and Country.

Anne K King
August 2021

---

[2] For reasons of clarity only, all the old boys whose stories are related in this account have been referred to as former pupils of NGS.

Introduction

When Great Britain declared war on Germany on 4th August 1914, the strength of the British Army, including reserves, was some 710,000 men, of whom only 80,000 were regular troops who could be said to be ready for war. The first Divisions of the British Expeditionary Force (BEF) embarked for France on 9th August and went into action for the first time on 23rd August, when they engaged the German Army at Mons. The subsequent German victory forced the BEF into retreat.

Lord Kitchener, the Secretary of State for War, calculated that the BEF would most likely suffer around 40% casualties in the first six months and that the war would continue for much longer than others anticipated. He believed hostilities would not 'be over by Christmas' but could take upwards of three years before they came to an end. Such a scenario would require far more troops than were available in the regular army.

In an effort to meet the expected shortage, in August 1914 Parliament issued a call for 100,000 men to enlist. The request was eagerly taken up and had reached a peak of 750,000 in early September. By the end of the First Battle of Ypres, fought during October and November 1914, many of the old professional army had been killed, as Kitchener had predicted, and the need for volunteer replacements was greater than ever.

It was during this early phase of recruitment that the many Pals battalions were formed. This practice saw recruits from similar towns, backgrounds or workplaces joining a particular battalion and fighting alongside friends and colleagues. Originally seen as a boost for recruitment, it was only when these battalions began to suffer very heavy casualties at the

First Battle of the Somme in 1916 that the devastating consequences on local areas became apparent and the formation of Pals battalions was discontinued.

By January 1915, around one million men from Britain and the Empire had volunteered but, with the number of casualties continuing to rise unabated, the need to replace them with new recruits became more urgent. The government were reluctant to introduce conscription, preferring to continue to rely on volunteers. With the aim of stimulating recruitment and discovering how many men might be available, the National Registration Act was introduced in 1915. The subsequent register indicated that some 5 million men aged between 15 and 65 were not in the forces. Many were in occupations considered important to the war effort, while others were unfit to serve through illness or disability. The remainder, around 1.5 million men, were encouraged to volunteer at public meetings or by propaganda, which often exaggerated tales of German atrocities. Despite these efforts, too few men came forward to meet the demand.

In a last-gasp attempt to increase the number of recruits and defer conscription, Lord Derby, the government's Director General of Recruitment, introduced his Group Scheme (more commonly called the Derby Scheme) on 16th October 1915. The plan was that volunteers registering under this scheme could continue to enlist for immediate service or could attest to their willingness to fight when called upon at a future date. Those who attested were placed in groups for call-up according to their age, taking the youngest first. All single men were to be called up before those who were married. In the intervening period between attestation and call-up, a man could return to his home and continue in his employment. He was issued with certification and an armband as proof that he had enlisted. This was a kind of moral conscription, in that it avoided men being seen by the general public as cowards who were unwilling to volunteer to fight. When large numbers of volunteers still failed to materialise, the Government declared that the last day for voluntary registration would be 15th December 1915 and that conscription would be introduced as quickly as possible after that date. The Military Service Bill, under which all single men between 16 and 41 were to be conscripted into the armed forces, was passed in January 1916 and came into effect on 2nd March. The Act was later extended to include married men up to the age of 50. It is estimated that by the end of the war, around 1,542,807 men had been conscripted.[3]

Some of the NGS men had belonged to the Territorial Force (TF) or to a university cadet corps before the war and were quick to enlist. Eight of those whose date of enlistment is on record and who were old enough volunteered within the first two months of the outbreak of war. Thirty-three men joined the Army; one later transferred to the Royal Flying Corps, while the remainder served in either the Royal or Merchant Navy.

By the end of 1914, Lord Kitchener's call to arms had been answered by 1,186,337 men, but the huge wave of patriotism posed problems for the regiments they rushed to join. Experienced soldiers would normally have been called upon to train new recruits, but the majority of these troops were now in France with the BEF. Additionally, there was a lack of accommodation in barracks for such large numbers and a dearth of equipment and uniforms with which to kit them out. Consequently, many recruits were posted to Reserve battalions for many months before they were mobilized and began their training.

---

[3] www.historyhit.com/conscription-in-world-war-one-explained

Three months of basic training were followed by several months of specialist training before a recruit could be considered ready to serve in the Army. When added to the time a man had already spent in Reserve, it could be well over a year from the date he signed up before a soldier was ready to join a Service battalion. Even then, many men arrived at the front unprepared for what they were about to face.

At the beginning of the war, a number of recruits remained on Home Service after they had completed their training. These soldiers were responsible for defending the country, should the need arise, and for training new recruits for eventual deployment overseas. As casualty rates rose, however, the demand for replacements at the front grew exponentially and the home service battalions became reliant on those who were considered to be unsuitable or unfit for service overseas.

The ages of the thirty-seven NGS men at the time of their deaths ranged between eighteen and thirty-five. They came from different backgrounds and were employed in a variety of trades and professions before they went off to war. Many were single, some were married and of those, a few were fathers. They fought in various theatres of war and in many different units on land, sea and in one case, in the air. Some enlisted, others were conscripted. They held various ranks and while some served for much of the war, others died within a few weeks of reaching the front. A large number were killed in action and their bodies never found. Of those who have known graves, some were buried by their comrades close to where they fell, while others died from their wounds, from illness or in accidents. Two died in England and are buried in private family plots in Rossendale.

Chapter 1

British troops first engaged the Germ? town of Mons on 23rd August 1914. The Germans ??????? strategic victory on the BEF, forcing them to retreat. In doing so, they were unable to prevent a German advance towards Paris which was not halted until the two sides lined up at the First Battle of the Marne in early September. Although a British victory, the battle saw the end of hopes for a quick, decisive conflict. Both sides began to dig in and the line of opposing trenches soon stretched from the Belgian coast almost as far as Switzerland. In between, it bulged out into a salient around the town of Ypres and ran in front of towns such as Reims, Soissons and Verdun before ending in Alsace, close to the Swiss border.

By the end of 1914, the BEF had suffered such huge casualties that their fighting strength had been severely depleted. The British army was now in desperate need of Kitchener's volunteers. The first of the NGS men began to reach the Western Front towards the end of 1914, by which time the war had developed into one of attrition. Troops from both sides had entered a period of trench warfare that was to last from September 1914 until the spring of 1918. Dug into these positions, the line remained more or less fixed, with little ground gained on either side.

It is possible that Edward Jackson was the first of the NGS men to go to war, although there is no way that this can be confirmed definitively. James Hutchinson enlisted a few weeks after Edward and he too embarked for France. This was not the destination for all of the early volunteers. The third history, that of James Tomlinson, illustrates the difficulties and suffering that men endured in a very different theatre of war: the Eastern Mediterranean.

2nd Lieutenant Edward Philips Jackson
3rd Battalion, Royal Warwickshire Regiment
Died 9th May 1915

Remembered
Le Touret Military Memorial
Pas de Calais, France

The Roll of Honour includes home town details and shows that Edward Jackson was not from Rossendale, or even from Lancashire. He came from the small Warwickshire village of Monks Kirby. According to the 1901 census, at that date he was living with his parents at 28 Lutterworth Road in Pailton and that is the address recorded in the NGS records[4] when he was admitted to the school on 30th April 1902.

So why was a boy who lived in Warwickshire being educated in Lancashire? In reporting his death, a Rossendale newspaper noted that Edward was the "nephew of Mr T E Jackson....headmaster of [the new] Bacup and Rawtenstall

---

Photograph: De Ruvigney's Vol 1 at archive.org - out of copyright
[4] These records were collated by former BRGS Headmaster P L Clark in his work on the Honour Roll which is held in the school archives

Secondary School."[5] Edward's father had decided that his son should be educated at his brother's school. The most usual age for admission was 11 or 12, but the school was prepared to take boys as young as 8.[6] T E Jackson was a bachelor who lived with his sister in the school house. Although far from home, Edward would be cared for by his aunt and uncle. He left NGS in 1908 to attend the prestigious Warwick School,[7] the fourth oldest Public School in England.

Additional information was found in De Ruvigny's Roll of Honour[8] and on the website for the Pailton War Memorial.[9] The second son of Reverend William and Mrs Mary Jackson, Edward was born on 11th December 1893 in Monks Kirby, Warwickshire, where his father was the vicar.

In October 1912, Edward went up to Trinity College Cambridge to read law and while there he developed a keen interest in the Territorial Force. He joined the college's Training Corps and on the outbreak of war immediately interrupted his studies to volunteer. He enlisted in the 3rd Battalion, Royal Warwickshire Regiment and was gazetted 2nd Lieutenant on 15th August.

The 3rd (Reserve) Royal Warwickshire Regiment was a training unit that remained in Britain throughout the war. Originally based in Warwick, it relocated to Portsmouth in August 1914 and later to the Isle of Wight. Having completed his training, Edward left for France on 25th December and on arrival he was attached to the 1st South Wales Borderers (SWB) as part of the reinforcements following their heavy losses.

---

[5] Rossendale Free Press: 22 May 1915 The new school opened in 1913

[6] 'Reflection of Life at NGS' by G Walmsley brgs.org.uk/ archive/1997

[7] Gerald Frykman, Warwick School archivist, confirmed that Edward was a pupil at the school from 1908-1912

[8] Entries can be viewed at www.ancestry.co.uk

[9] www.ww1wargraves.co.uk/ww1_cemeteries/memorials_pailton.asp

The war diary for the period describes life in the battalion.[10] The early months of 1915 were wet and cold, but despite heavy shelling from both sides there were periods of relative quiet along the front. Time was spent in training exercises, repairing communication lines and trenches, cleaning kit and equipment and making preparations for the next assault on enemy lines. Orders were received to move forward on 7th May but the attack was postponed and the battalion ordered to return to their billets. They marched out on the 8th and took up their positions in the reserve trench.

The fighting on 9th May was to become one of the British Army's worst disasters of the war. The Battle of Aubers Ridge had been planned as a pincer attack on German lines, with the allies launching a dual assault following a preliminary bombardment. However, Haig's Army was constrained by a shortage of artillery, as many of his guns were in Flanders at the Second Battle of Ypres. Additionally, the lack of ammunition, a problem since 1914, had now reached acute levels.

The preliminary bombardment started at 5am but only lasted 40 minutes. Enemy troops were observed watching from their trenches and, as soon as the ground attack commenced, they attacked the advancing infantry with heavy mortar and machine gun fire. Many were killed as they left the British trenches and those who made it out into No Man's Land were quickly cut down or impaled on the thick barbed wire entanglements, where they were picked off by enemy snipers and machine gunners. The British attack was called off at 6am.

Edward's battalion had been held in reserve. Ordered forward at 2.50pm, they found the dead and wounded from the first assault were blocking the way. The subsequent

---

[10] Nat Archives Ref WO 95/1280/3

confusion, combined with the strength of German resistance, delayed the second assault until 4pm. By then, the German guns had roared into action again and the British found themselves stranded, unable to advance or retreat.

The Battalion's casualties totalled 9 officers and 224 other ranks killed, wounded or missing, while the total casualties for the British were some 11,000 men. In relative terms, the Battle of Aubers Ridge had one of the highest casualty rates of the entire war. According to the war diary, it was during the battalion's second assault that Lt Jackson was killed.

Edward was 21 years old when he died. His body was never found but his name is engraved on the Le Touret Memorial within Richebourg L'Avoue Military Cemetery, Pas de Calais. He is also remembered at Trinity College, Cambridge, on the Pailton War Memorial, in St Editha's Church Monks Kirby and at Warwick School.

Le Touret Memorial

Private James Hutchinson
20th Battalion, Royal (City of London) Fusiliers
Died 23rd November 1915

Bethune Town Cemetery
Pas de Calais, France

James Hutchinson was born at 80 Burnley Road, Edenfield on the 19th of November 1887. The only son of Alice and John Hutchinson, he was the third of their four children and was known as Jim.[11] His father was a coal and lime merchant in Shuttleworth, a small hamlet between Edenfield and Bury. When the family moved to Rawtenstall they took up residence at 8 Queen's Terrace and John expanded his business to include trading as a corn merchant.

James's early schooling began at St Mary's School in Rawtenstall and he later progressed to Newchurch Grammar School where he was admitted on 2nd May 1899. After he completed his education, he started work as a clerk for his father. He was a member at St Mary's church in Rawtenstall

---

[11] Image and information: Rossendale Free Press: 11th December 1915

and sang in the choir. A keen member of the Boy Scout movement, he was well known and popular.[12]

The entry for James on the Commonwealth War Graves Commission (CWGC) database shows that he joined the 20th Battalion, Royal Fusiliers (City of London) as a Private and was issued with the service number 5098. This unit was a "Public School" battalion; one of the Pals' battalions formed for Kitchener's New Armies. In the beginning, the battalion was made up exclusively from former public school boys and membership was by application only. It proved to be so popular that four further Public School battalions were formed; three of these within the Royal Fusiliers.

As the war progressed and casualties mounted, the Army began to suffer from a severe shortage of trained officers. To remedy this, soldiers in the Public School battalions were openly encouraged to apply for commissions. With large numbers of them leaving to train as officers, the exclusivity of the battalions could not be sustained and the vacancies were filled by men from all walks of life.

The 20th Royal Fusiliers was formed at Epsom in September 1914 and was under the command of Lt Col C H Bennett. Recruits received their initial, basic training at camps near their homes with the various sections only amalgamating into the full battalion on 26th June 1915. From this date the battalion came under the command of the 33rd Division of Kitchener's 4th Army.

The division concentrated at Clipstone, near Mansfield, in July 1915 before moving to Salisbury Plain for advanced training and firing practice. On receipt of embarkation orders, the battalion began to move out on 12th November and the first units reached Boulogne two days later. By the 21st of the month, the Division had reached the concentration area

---

[12] http://www.rawtenstallwarmemorial.org.uk/files/page_25.html

around Morbeque in Northern France. Now part of the 19th Brigade, the 20th Royal Fusiliers were taken as far as Thiennes by train before they marched to their positions at Bethune.

James died on 23rd November 1915, a few days after his 28th birthday. No service record survives, but the 1921 publication Soldiers Died in the Great War states that he died from "wounds received in action."[13] The Manchester Evening News and the local paper both carried short reports of his death and the latter included a few brief details relating to his army service.[14] He had enlisted on 5th September 1914, only a few months after war was declared, and after training locally, had joined his battalion at their base in Epsom. Following a period of advanced training, he had embarked for France on 14th November 1915.

Not long after his son's departure for the front, Councillor Hutchinson received a letter from a Captain Yorston notifying him that his son had been wounded in action on 22nd November. Notification from the Infantry Records Office at Hounslow followed and confirmed that James had succumbed to his injuries and had died the following day.[15] He had been in France for eight days.

An entry in the battalion diary on 22nd November states that at 8.45am that day, men from C & D companies had been sent out to relieve their comrades in A & B companies in the front line trenches. While moving forward, two soldiers from C Company had been injured and one later died from his wounds.[16] It is reasonable to conclude that this dead soldier was James since records confirm that he was in the 20th battalion's C Company and Captain Yorston wrote that he had been wounded on the 22nd of the month.

---

[13] Published by HMSO 1921   Accessed at Ancestry UK
[14] Rossendale Free Press: 4th December 1915
[15] Ibid
[16] National Archives Ref WO95/2423

James lies in Plot IV.G.2 in Bethune Town Cemetery in the Pas de Calais department of Northern France. He is remembered on the Rawtenstall War Memorial and at St Mary's Church in the town. His name is also engraved on the Hutchinson family headstone in the churchyard at Edenfield, the village of his birth.

Bethune Town Cemetery

Chapter 2

Although the history of the fighting in France and Flanders during World War 1 receives a lot of attention, from late October 1914 until the end of October 1918, the Allied Powers were also engaged in a struggle against Macedonia, Serbia, Bulgaria and the mighty Ottoman Empire in the Eastern theatre of war. Perhaps the most infamous of these campaigns was in the Dardanelles, more commonly called the Gallipoli Landings or simply Gallipoli.

Allied troops had first landed on the peninsula, at Cape Helles and Anzac Cove, on 25th April 1915 with the aim of knocking Turkey out of the war and so gain a strategic advantage. After many weeks of fighting, and with casualties mounting, another landing was made on 5th August at Suvla Bay. This was an attempt to break the impasse but it quickly developed into chaos and deadlock.

The hope of breaking through to Constantinople and forcing the Ottoman Empire out of the war was never achieved. All three beachheads were overlooked by high ground controlled by a strong Ottoman force. The allied campaign quickly stagnated and the troops found themselves living and fighting in appalling conditions, pinned down by the Turks and unable to bury their dead who lay all around them. Entrenched in difficult and inhospitable terrain, they endured weeks of close combat fighting. The situation was further exacerbated by the extreme heat, insanitary conditions, swarms of flies and a dearth of fresh water all of which resulted in more troops being evacuated from Gallipoli suffering from disease than from injury. James Tomlinson fought and died on the peninsula.

2nd Lieutenant James Tomlinson
13th Battalion, Lancashire Fusiliers
Died 22nd November 1915

Azmak Cemetery
Suvla, Turkey

James Ashworth Tomlinson[17] was born in Stacksteads near Bacup on 26th March 1891 to James Tomlinson, a local Waterfoot blacksmith and wheelwright, and his wife Elizabeth. When his father died a year after his birth, Elizabeth, James and his elder sister went to live with Elizabeth's parents, Joshua and Frances Ashworth. James started school at Waterfoot Board School and joined NGS on 15th January 1903. His maternal grandmother died the following November and his mother and grandfather had moved to Southport by the date of the 1911 census. Discovering that Elizabeth had moved to Southport and knowing her middle name was Hannah made it possible to positively identify the correct soldier from among the 30 Tomlinson records in the Commonwealth War Grave Commission's (CWGC) database.

---

[17] Photograph: Rossendale Free Press 4th December 1915

When he left NGS, James started work in a local branch of the Lancashire and Yorkshire Bank, later transferring to their office at Shudehill, Manchester.[18] He joined up at Manchester on 4th September 1914, a few months after war was declared. He was 23 years of age and was issued with service number 10728. Only a few pages of his service record have survived [19] and these indicate that he joined the 18th (3rd City) Battalion, Manchester Regiment, [20] a Pals battalion composed of clerks and warehousemen. The following January, he was recommended for a commission but, in confirming that he thought him a suitable candidate, his Lieutenant Colonel added that there was no vacancy for him in the 18th battalion.

Having completed officer training and having been gazetted as a 2nd Lieutenant, James joined the 9th (Service) Battalion, Lancashire Fusiliers[21] and sailed from Liverpool on 5th July 1915, heading for the Dardanelles. He arrived at Suvla Bay on 6th August[22] and was posted to the Fusiliers' 1st battalion. Men of this unit had distinguished themselves on the first morning of the landings at Cape Helles on 25th April 1915, when they had won what was hailed in the Press as an impressive "six VCs before breakfast." The beach was later renamed Lancashire Landing in honour of the Fusiliers.

Officers suffered every bit as much as the other ranks in the appalling trench conditions on the peninsula and on 27th September the battalion diary noted that "2 Lieut (*sic*) Tomlinson sent sick."[23] He returned to duty on October 5th, just as a short period of calm came to an end. The war diary

---

[18] Liverpool Post & Daily Mercury and Yorkshire Post: both 1st Dec 1915
[19] National Archives Ref 399/38675
[20] One of the 8 'Pals' Battalions of the Manchester Regiment
[21] The London Gazette: 16th March 1915
[22] Yorkshire Post: 1 December 1915.
[23] 1st Battalion Lancashire Fusiliers war diary at Ancestry.co.uk

reported a rise in sniper attacks and the firing of gas bombs, the contents of which created "rather an unpleasant smell and stinging of the eyes." [24] During this time the 1st battalion were called upon to assist the Royal Engineers in laying wire entanglements and digging new trenches to the rear.

By November, the nights were becoming noticeably colder but the lines were quieter than normal, allowing time for training sessions. The diary entry on 21st/22nd November carried a report of an incident following one of these sessions and stated: *"1630. At the conclusion of the bombing instructions for officers held by the sergt major 2nd Royal Fusiliers, while the bombs were being put away, one mills bomb appears to have been accidently exploded. Three officers 1st Bn Lancashire Fus wounded, one later dying of the wound."(Sic)*[25]

Although the soldier is not named in the diary, a second record is more revealing. The daily casualty report for the 29th Division[26] confirms that only one officer was killed in the 24 hour period to 7pm on 22nd November. The casualty was named as 2nd Lieutenant J A Tomlinson, 1st Lancashire Fusiliers, who had "Died of Wounds." There are no other entries for anyone of that name in the month of November, confirming that the officer killed in the training accident was James.

At the time he was killed, James Tomlinson was 24 years old and had been in the army for little more than a year. He is buried in plot II.F.21 at Azmak Cemetery in Suvla. To contend with the landslide-prone ground, the grave markers are in the form of small stone pedestals rather than the taller and heavier, upright headstones found in the CWGC cemeteries of Northern France and Flanders.

---

[24] 1st Battalion Lancashire Fusiliers war diary at Ancestry.co.uk
[25] Ibid
[26] Available at the National Archives - accessed through Ancestry

A copy of the War Office telegram sent to Mrs Tomlinson is held in the Officer's Long Number Papers held at Kew.[27] Dated 26th November, it makes no mention of the explosion, only stating that James "died of wounds received in action." This was not atypical; telegrams often held little information as to cause of death, simply stating "killed in action" or "died of wounds." Understandably, more personal letters to next of kin from commanding officers tended to soften the blow by claiming their loved one had "died instantly" or "didn't suffer", whether this was the case or not.

The Rossendale Free Press reported that *"the late officer was particularly well known in the Waterfoot and Rawtenstall districts."*[28] While resident in Waterfoot, James had been connected with St James the Great Parish Church and had taught in the Sunday school. He was also a member of the Church of England Men's Society.

Obituaries were published in the Liverpool Post & Daily Mercury and the Yorkshire Post. James is remembered on the Civic War Memorial in Southport, at the town's St James the Great Parish Church and on the Lancashire & Yorkshire Bank Memorial. The Bank memorial has since been lost.

Headstone - Azmak Cemetery Suvla

---

[27] National Archives Ref WO339/38675
[28] Rossendale Free Press: 4th December 1915

Chapter 3

With the German advance halted after the Battle of the Marne and the two belligerents facing each other from their opposing trenches, the Western Front became the main focus of the war for much of the next four years. Between 1915 and 1917, many offensives were fought in both France and Flanders but little was gained by either side and the stalemate continued.

The Great War was markedly different from conflicts of earlier centuries both in the way in which it was fought and in the enormous number of casualties that resulted. Some major attacks were preceded by a massive artillery bombardment lasting hours, or even days, when high explosive and shrapnel shells would rain down on the enemy positions. Thousands of men were involved in each of these battles. After going "over the top" and out into No Man's Land, troops had to negotiate multiple barbed wire entanglements while coming under attack from enemy shell, sniper and machine gun fire.

After 1915, the use of chlorine, phosgene and mustard gas was not uncommon. The Germans first used poison gas, with devastating effect, during the 2nd Battle of Ypres in April 1915. Conversely, Britain's first gas attack, at Loos in September of that year, was disastrous. The effectiveness of a gas attack is dependent on the wind carrying the gas over enemy lines. At Loos, the wind conditions were unfavourable and the gas hung over No Man's Land before it drifted back towards British lines and into the faces of the unsuspecting troops.

At the beginning of the war, armies still raised cavalry regiments and relied on teams of horses to move supplies, ammunition and artillery pieces. Four years later, due to a rapid increase in technological innovation, war was highly mechanised, as evidenced by the introduction of motor transport, aircraft and tanks.

In Flanders, the focus of much of the fighting was around the town of Ypres, a major allied stronghold that bulged out into German-held territory and blocked their way to the coast. If this salient could be captured, it would allow the Germans to advance to the channel ports, cut the Allies off from their major supply routes to the Western Front and so bring an end to the war. During the second Battle of Ypres, fought between 22nd April and 25th May 1915, the Germans failed in their attempt to capture the town. The heavy shelling before and during this attack left much of Ypres in ruins. Although the Allies retained control of the town, some higher ground in the Salient was lost, allowing enemy artillery to move even closer to British-held positions.

The Ruined Cloth Hall in Ypres[29]

The winter of 1915/16 was so severe that it brought fighting to a temporary halt until spring, when the Germans continued their attack and secured one of the last high points,

---

[29] By kind permission of The Keasbury-Gordon Photograph Archive

known to the Allies as "The Bluff".[30] The Germans now held most of the high positions overlooking allied positions around Ypres.

Away from Flanders, in early 1916 preparations were being made for a major allied offensive on the Somme. The aim was to ease pressure on the French at Verdun, by deflecting German attention northwards. As a result of forcing the Germans into extending their front line, their troops would be spread more thinly, with a consequent reduction in defensive capability. This in turn would allow the Allies to break through German lines and so bring an end to the war. The Battle of the Somme was to be a baptism of fire for many of the men of Lord Kitchener's New Army, the majority of whom were totally inexperienced and lacked the high level of training of a pre-war regular soldier.

Four of the NGS old boys died on the Western Front during 1916, one of them in Flanders and three on the Somme. Two of them have no known grave.

---

[30] This wooded ridge ran beside the Ypres–Comines Canal, SE of Ypres, and was the location of considerable mining and tunnelling by both sides

Private Alan Booth
10th Battalion, West Yorkshire Regiment
Died 3rd March 1916

Lijssenthoek Military Cemetery
Belgium

Alan Booth[31] was born in Sunk Island, near Hull on 13th October 1897, one of seven children born to Jane and James Booth. James was a school master who had moved to a number of different schools during his career. He first moved to Hensall cum-Heck in West Yorkshire before taking up a post in Lancashire. The family lived at 1142 Burnley Road in the small Lancashire village of Water. According to the CWGC register, Alan's parents later moved to 3 Richmond Grove, Levenshulme, Manchester.

On 7th September 1910, Alan was enrolled at Newchurch Grammar School and after he had completed his education, he joined the Lancashire & Yorkshire Bank, working as a junior clerk at the Waterfoot branch. He was a regular attender at Lumb church and sang in the choir.

---

[31] Photograph: Rossendale Free Press 11th March 1916

Alan's service papers have not survived but some relevant information was found in local newspapers and on military websites. Having enlisted at Rawtenstall on 6th February 1915, Private 18057 Booth served as a signaller in the 10th battalion of the West Yorkshire Regiment (Prince of Wales Own). After 4 months' training, he embarked for France and by June was serving in Flanders.[32]

In March 1916, the Manchester Evening News reported that Alan's father had received word that his son had been seriously wounded by shell fragments in the arm and chest[33] and a few days later the Rossendale Free Press informed its readers that a Lieutenant in the regiment had written to advise Mr Booth that the doctor held out very little hope of a recovery. The officer went on to say that Private Booth was one of his best men, *"always cheerful and plucky"* and hoped that Mr Booth would not think his letter unfeeling, but the fact was that he had not much time to write as *"shells were constantly bursting all around them."*[34] By the time this news was published in the local press, Alan had succumbed to his injuries.

The West Yorkshire regiment that Alan joined was part of the 50th Brigade, 17th Division of the British Expeditionary Force that had landed in France on 13th July, 1915. The Division's original orders were that they would be retained for home defence but this was subsequently amended to overseas service due to the Army's desperate need for trained reinforcements. Advance parties left for France on 6th July, while embarkation for the bulk of the troops began on the 12th of the month. On their arrival, troops underwent an initial period of trench familiarisation in France before they moved into Belgium to hold part of the front line in the southern area of the Ypres salient.

---

[32] Rossendale Free Press: 11th March 1916
[33] Manchester Evening News: 8th March 1916
[34] Rossendale Free Press: 11th March 1916

In the absence of a service record, the unit war diary has been used to create a picture of Alan's day to day life in the battalion in the days before he died.[35] Positioned in dugouts at Kruisstraat about 7 miles from Ypres, and having suffered heavy enemy shelling in the early days of January 1916, the battalion spent the rest of that month undergoing inspections, drills and general training. They took part in bombing (grenade) practice and constructed a rifle range. On 26th February all was quiet until about 5pm, when the British lines came under a heavy enemy bombardment.

The battalion later moved to Oosthoek,[36] east of Ypres and at 4.30 am on the 2nd March commenced an attack on trenches previously lost to the enemy. After these were successfully retaken, they moved forward to attack the German front line trenches. For the remainder of that day the British troops came under continuous heavy retaliatory fire which resulted in around 120 casualties.

When Mr Booth received notification of Alan's death, he was advised that his son had died as a result of wounds received while under heavy shell fire. The Register of Soldiers' Effects[37] shows that he was treated at No 10 Casualty Clearing Station (CCS)[38] near Poperinghe, but died from his injuries on 3rd March 1916. He was 18 years old.

About six months after their son's death, Mr & Mrs Booth received a letter from a Private Bairstow who had served in Alan's regiment.[39] He wrote from Lake Hospital, Ashton-under-Lyne where he was recovering from injuries and shell shock following the Battle of the Somme. He wrote, he said, in the hope of comforting them.

---

[35] National Archives Ref WO95/2004/1
[36] Today this area is known as Westhoek
[37] National Army Museum – accessed at Ancestry
[38] No10 CCS was at Remy Sidings from July '15 to April '18
[39] Private 11686, George Bairstow

"*As your late son Alan's pal, I am writing this to let you know something of his life in Belgium and France. We were at St Eloi at the time and we two were together for a fortnight at a signal station in a wood just behind the trenches. . . . . At the time of the Battle of Loos our battalion did 23 days in the trenches without a break. Then we moved over the frontier to Steenvoorde for a rest. We both had a good time there and Alan's knowledge of French came in very useful. . . . . when in Ypres we were always exploring the town if we had nothing else to do. He could never see danger, and consequently we got into some hot places at times. In fact, he delighted in taking unnecessary risks. He was a very clever signaller, and certainly deserved promotion. . . . . Towards the end of February . . . . . . .Alan was signalling at headquarters about half a mile in the rear and I was in the front line, but I used to see him when I went for rations at night. The last time I saw Alan was about 2am on 2nd March. He was on duty at the instrument at the time. . . . . .On the 8th March we moved back for a rest and then I heard of Alan's death. It seemed like the last straw and for some time I never even wrote home. . . . . .No one ever had a better pal and everyone liked him. He was so manly and unselfish.*"[40]

Private Alan Booth lies in Plot IV.D.47A in Lijssenthoek Military Cemetery in Belgium. During the war the village was situated on the main rail communication line between the Ypres battlefields and military bases in the rear. Close to the Front, but out of range of most German field artillery, a number of casualty clearing stations were built there. The cemetery grew up next to the casualty units and was first used by the French, but from June 1915 it began to be used by Commonwealth forces.[41] Lijssenthoek is now the second largest Commonwealth Cemetery in Belgium after Tyne Cot Cemetery, with a total of 10,754 burials.

Alan is remembered on the Men of Lumb War Memorial currently housed in Whittaker Museum, Whittaker Park in

---

[40] Bacup Chronicle: 23rd September 1916 - Edited extract
[41] CWGC.com

Rawtenstall. His name was engraved on the Lancashire & Yorkshire Bank Memorial at the branch in King Street, Manchester, but as a result of bank mergers this has now been lost.

Lijssenthoek Military Cemetery

Alan Booth's Headstone

Chapter 4

Much has been written about the first Battle of the Somme. The campaign lasted over four months, from 1st July until 18th November 1916 and resulted in a combined casualty rate of over 1,000,000 men 300,000 of whom were killed. The following paragraphs are not intended as a concise history of the Battle of the Somme, or even of the first day of the battle. To attempt to do so would not only be an impossible task but would understate and trivialize its importance.

By early 1916, plans were underway for a major Franco-British attack along the Western Front. The Somme was chosen because this was the point on the Western Front where the French and British armies met. The original plan had been for the French to take command, with Britain in a support role. Following the German attack on French positions at Verdun in February 1916, however, France had to concentrate the majority of her troops further south, leaving only a few divisions on the Somme, insufficient strength to lead the proposed attack. In these circumstances Britain, with the support of thousands of troops from across her Empire, would now take the leading role in the campaign.

The date for the commencement of the attack was set for 30th June but following heavy rain, was delayed until 1st July. In the week leading up to zero hour, German lines were bombarded 24 hours a day and more than 1,700,000 shells were fired during that period. It was thought that the artillery barrage would be so intense that it would cut the wire in front of the German lines, destroy their trenches and dugouts and leave no one in the area alive to oppose the British troops as they walked forward towards the German positions.

What occurred on the first day of the battle was very different. Although the bombardment was the largest and longest ever seen at the time, many of the shells failed to explode. Those that did were later discovered to have been the wrong type; exploding high in the air rather than at ground level and so failing to cut the wire entanglements as had been expected. The German dugouts were well constructed and made of concrete and survived mostly unscathed. They extended many feet underground and had large galleries where troops could shelter safely, if uncomfortably, from the onslaught above.

Part of the British pre-planning had been to dig a series of nineteen mines, packed with explosives, under German lines. The plan was to detonate them at 7.28 am, 2 minutes before zero hour, at which time the infantry advance would begin and allied troops could use the resultant craters as cover. Despite the arranged timetable, the commander at Hawthorn Ridge Redoubt, Lieutenant-General Sir Aylmer Hunter-Weston, ordered that the mine there be detonated at 7.20am as he feared the advancing troops could be buried by falling debris. By taking this step he gave the enemy advance notice that the attack was about to begin.

At 7.30am on the 1st July, officers' whistles blew all along the line to alert the British and Commonwealth troops that it was time for the first wave to go over the top. As they did so, the forewarned Germans climbed out of their undamaged bunkers, set up their machine guns and began firing. Many allied soldiers were cut down as soon as they left the British trenches and those that were able to proceed further found the majority of the wire was uncut with only a few gaps here and there. As men queued up to file through, the German machine gunners concentrated their fire on the gaps and scythed them down. Many of the wounded were left entangled in the wire and were targeted by German snipers while their comrades struggled to proceed under a hail of gunfire and shells. Battle plans soon developed into chaos.

Some of the battalions who did manage to advance towards their objectives found the expected support on their flanks had been held up or, in many cases wiped out, forcing them back to the shelter of their front line trenches. Many casualties occurred during this retreat. Seeing that the first wave had failed to make progress, British commanders sent in their second and then third waves, only to see them meet a similar fate.

The expected allied walk to victory turned into the worst day in the history of the British Army. At roll call that evening British casualties totalled 57,470 men, 19,240 of whom had been killed. Three were NGS men. The Battle of the Somme dragged on until 18th November when, with the arrival of winter and having secured minimal gains, the British High Command decided to call a halt. By the time the campaign foundered in mud in the middle of November, casualties on both sides amounted to more than a million men.

Troops going over the top, Somme 1916[42]

---

[42] By kind permission of The Keasbury-Gordon Photograph Archive

2nd Lieutenant Ernest Jackson
9th Battalion, Lancashire Fusiliers
Died 1st July 1916

Remembered
Thiepval Memorial

Ernest[43] was born in October 1890, the second youngest of six children born to John Jackson, a lamplighter, and his wife Mary. The family lived at 31 Todmorden Road, Bacup.[44] Ernest was admitted to Newchurch Grammar School as a Springfield Scholar on 23 January 1902. He then went to Rochdale Grammar School before proceeding to Manchester University in 1906. He graduated with a B.A. in French and Flemish in 1910.[45] A gifted linguist, Ernest was employed as a teacher and assistant headmaster at Tynemouth Municipal High School until 1913, when he moved to Leeds Modern School as a Languages Master. On 23rd December 1915 he married fellow teacher, Lillian Tunnicliffe, at St Aiden's Church in Leeds.

---

[43] Photograph: Bacup Times 15th July 1916
[44] WW1 papers collated by the late Philip Lane Clark - BRGS archive
[45] WW1.manchester.ac.uk/roll-of-honour/ernest-jackson/

Ernest Jackson's file at the National Archives shows that he enlisted at Leeds on 10th April 1915. He was posted to the Rifle Brigade on 18th April and began his training. He was discharged on 7th June, having been accepted for officer training. He joined the 3rd Battalion, Lancashire Fusiliers and was gazetted 2nd Lieutenant on 5th June 1915.[46]

Unfortunately for researchers, the long number papers for WW1 officers were extensively pruned in the 1930s and what remains today is sometimes very basic information. In Ernest's case the majority of the papers relate to the period after his death but there is a little information about his war service.

Once his officer training had been completed, he was posted to the 9th Lancashire Fusiliers and embarked for France on 22nd May 1916. Due to his excellent linguistic skills, he initially worked as a translator with the Belgian and French armies before he was attached to the 15th Battalion Lancashire Fusiliers (the 1st Salford Pals), just before the Battle of the Somme. The 1st July 1916, the first day of the Somme, would be remembered as the bloodiest day in the history of the British Army.

Although the Salford Pals had been in France since November, the Somme was to be their first real experience of battle and they were given the difficult task of attacking the heavily defended Thiepval Ridge. In July 1916 the village of Thiepval consisted of about a hundred buildings, and the Germans had turned it into a fortress. Over 30 machine gun emplacements were positioned around the village, each with commanding views of the slopes up which the British troops would have to attack. The week-long artillery bombardment prior to 1st July had failed to cut the German wire, and although many of the buildings in the village had been

---

[46] Officer Long Number Papers – National Archives Ref WO 339/43178

demolished by shellfire, most had deep, easily defended cellars into which the Germans had retreated. Even from these positions, they still had a clear view of the British lines below them.

On the morning of 1st July, the Lancastrians left their trenches and started up the slope, searching frantically for any breaks in the German wire. Almost immediately, they came under intense fire from the enemy machine guns above them. Only a few survived the onslaught, but about an hour after the attack began, air observers reported that there had been sightings of isolated parties of British troops entering the village. Thinking Thiepval had been taken, the British commanders called a halt to the artillery barrage. This allowed German gunners to turn their full attention to the allied trenches, which now came under extremely heavy attack.

Although a few men in the first wave reached the German lines *"not one man or officer from the Salford Pals who got there would live to tell the tale."*[47] Despite valiant efforts, all those who followed in later waves met much the same fate, ensuring Thiepval remained in German hands. It had proved to be an impregnable fortress. Ernest went missing during the assault on the ridge.

On 6th November 2013, the Manchester Evening News printed a memorial report of the attack. Ernest's battalion had been more or less wiped out in the first few hours. Of the 24 officers and 650 men who made the attack on Thiepval, 21 officers and 449 men became casualties. It was with a heavy heart that the Salford Pals' commander, Lieutenant Colonel John Henry Lloyd, wrote: *"I had a fine lot of officers and men….. I never saw a battalion during all my experience which was better. At 7.30 we started by 8.30 we were finished"* [48]

---

[47] 'Salford Pals' by Michael Steadman
[48] Manchester Evening News: 6th November 2013

Ernest's parents received the first official news in a telegram from the War Office dated 10th July. It was simply addressed to 'The Occupier' and advised that 2nd Lt Jackson had been reported missing as at 6th July. Mr Jackson advised Ernest's wife by telegram and the next day she received confirmation in a letter from her husband's commanding officer. A second communication from the War Office was received on the 2nd August. This amended the date of Ernest's disappearance from 6th to 1st July but gave no indication as to what might have happened to him.

Ernest was 26 years old. His body was never recovered and his name is engraved on the Thiepval Memorial to the Missing. He is also remembered on the family gravestone in Bacup Cemetery,[49] the Leeds City Council Education Department's Memorial[50] and at Manchester University.

Thiepval Memorial [51]

---

[49] Bacup Cemetery - Gen E 341
[50] Currently housed in the City Council Offices, George Street, Leeds
[51] Photograph: The War Graves Photographic Project

Rifleman Albert Aspden
16th Battalion, King's Royal Rifle Corps
Died 15th July 1916

Caterpillar Valley Cemetery
Longueval, France

Albert,[52] the youngest of Arthur and Hannah Aspden's three sons, was born on 1st June 1891 in the small East Lancashire mill town of Church, near Accrington. His father was a power loom overlooker, employed in a local cotton mill. When Arthur began working at Messrs Thorpe & Co's Laund Mill on Lee Brook Road in Rawtenstall, the family moved to the town and took up residence at 167 Cribden View, Burnley Road. Young Albert was a pupil at Constable Lee National School before he was admitted to Newchurch Grammar School on 15th January 1903. By the time he was 19, he was working as an office clerk for his father, who was by then a partner in Laund Mill.[53] Albert was a regular attender at St Paul's Church, Constable Lee where he sang in the choir. He

---
[52] Photograph: Bacup Chronicle 5th August 1916
[53] 1911 census records accessed at Ancestry

was also a member of St Mary's Church Lads' Brigade and secretary of the Junior Conservative League for a number of years, where he was said to have been an "ardent worker" on their behalf.[54]

Albert's military service record has survived. He joined up a few months after war was declared, enlisting at Rawtenstall on 9th October 1914. Called up for duty at Denham near Uxbridge on 19th of October, he was posted as Rifleman C929 to the 16th Battalion, King's Royal Rifle Corps (KRRC).

The 16th Battalion (Church Lads' Brigade) was formed at Denham in September 1914 by Field-Marshall Lord Grenfell, Governor of the Church Lads' Brigade (CLB). Grenfell had sent out an appeal to current and past members of the Brigade asking that those who had not already enlisted should join his regiment. Within a month of the raising of the battalion, Albert had enlisted. This might have been as a result of Grenfell's call to arms, since Albert was in the CLB, although there is nothing to confirm this was the case.

After basic training, the battalion underwent three months' advanced training in trench construction and by summer of 1915 they were waiting for their embarkation orders. They left England on 15th November and joined the Reserve. By June, final preparations were being made for the attack on the Somme, although the 16th King's Royal Rifles were not called upon until 15th July, when they attacked High Wood.

High Wood had been attacked on 14th July but, meeting increasing German resistance, troops had been unable to hold it. The 16th KRRC were part of the reinforcements brought up for the second attempt to take the wood. According to the battalion war diary, preparations began on the day before, when picks and shovels were withdrawn from the stores along with 200 rounds of ammunition and 2 sandbags per

---

[54] Rossendale Free Press: 5th August 1916

man. They arrived at their positions around 9.15pm and dug in. The lines were heavily shelled overnight.[55]

At 8.30am on 15th July, allied artillery bombarded enemy lines before the infantry moved forward towards High Wood at 9am. They were to attack the German lines, but this objective was uphill and over open ground. Before they had gone far, many were cut down by enfilade[56] fire and those who survived had to retreat. Many more attempts were made throughout the day, each one resisted by the enemy. A few men did reach the wood, but they were unable to drive out the Germans. By evening it was clear that the attack had failed and High Wood was evacuated. The 16th battalion lost one hundred and twenty men on 15th July. Among them was Rifleman Albert Aspden.

Announcing his death, the local newspaper noted that Albert was *"well-known and highly respected in the district."* The Company Sergeant Major wrote to Albert's parents to say their son had gone to help a wounded comrade and was most probably shot by a sniper. Albert *"was very popular in the platoon, had done good work and would be much missed."* The CSM ended by saying Albert's commanding officer had been pleased with his work and would have written personally, had he not been killed in the same attack.[57]

Albert had written home three days before he died saying they were going to *"put an end to Fritz,"* but added that if he fell, he would die *"as an Englishman does – fighting – and not as a conscientious objector."* [58] Although he was unaware of it, this letter proved to be Albert's valedictory speech and gives a valuable insight into his thoughts. Despite being a religious

---

[55] National Archives Ref WO 95/2430/3
[56] Sweeping gunfire directed along the length, rather than the breadth, of a line of troops
[57] Bacup Chronicle: 5th August 1916
[58] Bacup Chronicle: 5th August 1916

man, he appears to have disapproved of conscientious objectors, many of whom cited religious beliefs as their reason for refusing to fight.

After numerous attempts, and with enormous losses on both sides, it took the British three months to capture High Wood.[59] Historians suggest that the remains of some 8,000 British and German casualties may still lie there today.[60] Sadly, any attempt to recover them is considered too dangerous, due to the large amount of unexploded ordnance that still litters the ground over one hundred years after the battle.

Albert's body was recovered and is buried in plot XVI.D.35 at Caterpillar Valley Cemetery, near Longueval. The village is a short distance from High Wood. His name is also on the War Memorial in St Paul's Church and on the Rawtenstall Municipal War Memorial.

Albert Aspden's Headstone
Caterpillar Valley Cemetery

---

[59] Lost again during the German Spring Offensive in April 1918, it was retaken by the Allies in August 1918
[60] WW1battlefields.co.uk/somme/highwood

Private John Percy Turnbull
2/5th Battalion, Lancashire Fusiliers
Died 9th September 1916

Remembered Thiepval Memorial
Somme, France

John,[61] known to his immediate family as Percy, was born at Green's, in the hills above Stacksteads, on 2nd May 1889. He was the fifth son, and sixth child, of William and Mary Turnbull. William, a calico printer, owned Irwell Bank Printworks. In 1881, he founded Messrs Turnbull & Stockdale Ltd and became the company's managing director. By 1901 the family were living at Fernclough, a substantial family house in the small community of Stubbins near Ramsbottom. The house was close to Turnbull & Stockdale's Rosebank Print Works.

Percy began his schooling at Stacksteads National School and was enrolled at Newchurch Grammar School on 20th January 1897. It is unclear how long he studied at Newchurch before he joined his elder brother Benjamin as a pupil at New

---

[61] Photograph by kind permission of Philip Dunne, great nephew

College, a boarding school in Harrogate.[62] On leaving school, Percy studied at Cheshire Agricultural College and then joined the family business as managing director of the Chatterton Weaving Company Ltd, a subsidiary of Turnbull & Stockdale Ltd.[63] As an adult, he was a keen sports enthusiast and member of the local Conservative Association and the family were regular attenders at St Paul's Church in Ramsbottom.

A search at the National Archives discovered that none of Percy Turnbull's service papers have survived although there is a medal index card that confirms his regiment, battalion and service number. Some personal information has been gathered from a conversation with his great nephew[64] and from local newspaper accounts of his death.[65] Percy was called up at the end of February 1916. It appears that, since he had received both a grammar school and a private school education, he was offered a commission. He refused this in favour of a posting into the ranks as an ordinary soldier and joined the 2/5th battalion of the Lancashire Fusiliers with the service number 4892.[66]

Percy was called up around the time that plans for the attack on the Somme were being finalised. Allied commanders had appreciated that an enormous number of troops would be required for the campaign but they did not anticipate the high number of casualties that had occurred in the months before the attack. The urgent requirement to bring the army back up to full strength may explain why many recruits were sent out to France a matter of months after they had been called up.

---

[62] This independent school is now called Ashville College
[63] Percy's father was Chairman of the Chatterton Weaving Company
[64] Conversations with J Phillip Dunne, Percy's great nephew
[65] Manchester Evening News
[66] BuryArchivesonline.co.uk/soldier-records undated newspaper extract

At the beginning of the war, troops often took months to complete basic training. This was then enhanced with specialist training before they left Britain and continued when they reached their Service battalions. Many of the troops who were about to fight in the Battle of the Somme were in Kitchener's New Army and, not having had the benefit of extended training, arrived at the front very inexperienced.

Percy embarked for France in July 1916, four months after he joined the army. Like many of his comrades, and through no fault of his own, he was probably ill-prepared for the enormity of the task before him. Although his service record has been lost, reading the contents of the 2/5th Lancashire Fusiliers' war diary for the months of July to September 1916 encapsulates Percy's life in the battalion during that time.

The diary records that while they were in trenches south of Arras, two drafts of reinforcements arrived in early July; one on the 6th and another on the 15th.[67] Percy had left England in early July and so it is possible he was in one or other of these drafts. At the end of the month the battalion left Arras and moved down to the Somme where they took up their position near the village of Longueval. Although not involved in the early weeks of the Somme battle that had resulted in heavy casualties, the part they played was to prove every bit as costly.

Their arrival coincided with a period of relative calm and this allowed time for a little training, particularly in methods of attack, but by August their lines were almost constantly under attack from German artillery. During this time, a number of officers were killed or seriously wounded by active sniper attacks.[68] When darkness fell, the men were kept busy carrying ammunition to the various dumps to ensure that a

---

[67] National Archives Ref WO 95/2923/2
[68] Officers were easily identifiable from their uniform and were prime targets for enemy snipers.

steady supply of munitions was available for their own artillery. This activity was interspersed with time spent in the reserve trenches, but the periods of calm were now few and far between.

The battalion moved into trenches in front of Ginchy on 7th September in preparation for another major attack. At 3.20 in the morning of the 8th, they moved forward to a position to the east of Trones Wood where they relieved the North Lancashire Regiment. The village of Ginchy was in enemy hands and sat at the junction of six roads. If it could be captured, it would deprive the Germans of the observation posts overlooking the battlefield, from where they continually fired on allied positions.

The operation began on 9th September. It opened up with an intense British artillery bombardment at 4.45pm before troops moved forward into the attack at 5.30pm. The late hour had been specifically chosen to ensure darkness would fall before the Germans were able to mount a counter-attack. The 2/5th Lancashire Fusiliers were to go forward in the second wave. When the time came to go into the attack, they found that the troops involved in the first wave had been slow to vacate their jumping-off trenches and so, as the second wave moved forward on schedule, they found their entry into the trenches blocked by remnants of the first wave. Left out in the open, they came under intense enemy fire and suffered many casualties. Worse was to come. Moving out of the British lines they aimed for the wrong trench and, in the confusion, halted in a line of shell holes where there was little real protection. They now came under heavy enemy artillery and machine gun fire which slowed any attempt to advance. Faced with mounting casualties, the battalion withdrew just before sunset to consolidate their ranks.

At battalion roll call that evening, 16 out of 19 officers and 334 other ranks had been killed or wounded, or were listed as missing. Percy was one of the missing. He was 27 years old and had been at the front for only a matter of weeks before he was killed at the battle of Ginchy. If his body was ever recovered, it remained unidentified.

Percy's name is engraved on the Thiepval Memorial. It remembers over 72,000 British and South African servicemen who died in the Somme sector up until 20th March 1918 but who have no known grave. He is also remembered on Harrogate's Ashville College Memorial. A memorial window to both Percy and his father was installed in the family church of St Paul's in Ramsbottom.

Thiepval Memorial Inscription

Chapter 5

The First World War was not exclusively a land conflict. Both the Royal and Merchant Navies, and later the Royal Flying Corps, were instrumental in the ultimate victory over the Central Powers. For centuries, the British Navy had dominated the seas, but in the years leading up to the outbreak of war, Germany had attempted to contest this British superiority. The struggle ultimately led to a naval arms race between the two powers but, despite Germany's efforts, Britain maintained her naval supremacy and when war broke out she still had the most powerful navy in the world under the command of Admiral John Jellicoe.

Soon after war broke out, the Royal Navy began a naval blockade of Germany and her allies, thus cutting them off from essentials such as fuel, food and military supplies. By 1915, Germany was deploying submarines to attack allied shipping in a counter-effort to cut Britain off from her supply routes. Although German submarines proved effective against British merchant ships, in contrast to the situation in WW2, they were of limited effectiveness against navy ships.

Despite the might and preparedness of the Royal Navy, only one major sea battle, the Battle of Jutland, was fought during the whole of the Great War and this was indecisive. *"Many in the navy longed for decisive action and a great naval victory to recall the Battle of Trafalgar"*[69] and they were frustrated by what they perceived as inaction.

Four men from the school joined naval units during the war, one of whom died at the Battle of Jutland.

---

[69] www.bl.uk/world-war-one/articles/the-war-at-sea

Ordinary Seaman Tom Fielding
Royal Navy
Died 31ˢᵗ May 1916

Remembered
Plymouth Naval Memorial

Tom Fielding[70] was born in Rawtenstall on 6ᵗʰ April 1898. He was the son of Thomas, a piano tuner, and his wife Elizabeth. The couple had two other children; a daughter two years older and a son two years younger than Tom. The family lived at 10 St Mary's Place, Rawtenstall. When Elizabeth died in 1902, Thomas remarried within the year and had a child by his second wife, Catherine, in 1904. Thomas Snr died in August 1910, leaving his widow to bring up their son, Tom and his two siblings. First educated at St Mary's C of E School in Rawtenstall, Tom went to Newchurch Grammar School on a scholarship and was admitted to the register on 8ᵗʰ September 1909. A slight boy, only a couple of inches over 5 feet, he joined the Navy straight from school.

---

[70] Photograph: Rossendale Free Press 10ᵗʰ June 1916

As D/32495 Fielding, Tom joined the Navy with the rank of Boy 2nd class[71] and was posted to HMS *Powerful*, a boys' land-based training ship at Devonport, on 9th December 1914. On 10th January 1915 he was transferred to HMS *Impregnable*, another boys' training base, and four days later was promoted to the rank of Boy 1st class.[72] He was said to have been a bright lad and during his training he won a great number of prizes.[73] Having completed his training, he joined his first seagoing vessel, HMS *Invincible*, on the 23rd June 1915. His navy record can be viewed at the National Archives and indicates his rank was amended to 'Ordinary Seaman' when he reached his eighteenth birthday.[74]

Invincible was built in 1907. She was the world's first battlecruiser and the lead ship of three in her class in the Royal Navy. After a collision with a submarine in 1913, she was in dock undergoing repairs and a planned major refit when war was declared. She was returned to operational duties in August 1914 despite the fact that some of her refit enhancements were incomplete.

In April 1916, *Invincible* sailed to Scapa Flow to undertake a course of gunnery practice. Shortly after her arrival, the entire Grand Fleet received orders to prepare to engage with the German Navy off Denmark's Jutland Peninsula. On 30th May, Admiral Jellico led sixteen battleships and three battlecruisers eastwards, out of Scapa Flow. Tom Fielding was going to war.

The following day, *Invincible* went into action by opening fire on an enemy cruiser. She was observed to have made several direct hits on the vessel before turning to engage the

---

[71] The rank on entry to a RN training establishment for boys aged 15 - 17
[72] A boy aged 16 - 18 who had served 9 - 18 months as a Boy2, who had shown sufficient proficiency and had at least one good conduct badge
[73] Tom Fielding's entry on the website rawtenstallwarmemorial.org.uk
[74] He is listed as 'Boy 1st Class' on the Plymouth Naval War Memorial

leading German battlecruiser. Before she could do so, two vessels in the German fleet fired three salvoes and at least one 12-inch shell struck *Invincible* amidships. The shell penetrated her front turret, blew off the roof and detonated one of the magazines. The subsequent explosion blew the ship in half and she sank within seconds. Only six of her crew of 1,031 officers and men were picked up, one of whom had been in the turret and was blown into the sea.

An eyewitness account of the attack was given by the senior surviving officer. "*The Ship had been hit several times by heavy shell, but no appreciable damage had been done when at 6.34 p.m. a heavy shell struck "Q" turret and, bursting inside, blew the roof off. This was observed from the control top. Almost immediately following there was a tremendous explosion amidships indicating that "Q" magazine had blown up. The ship broke in half and sank in 10 or 15 seconds. The survivors, on coming to the surface, saw the bow and stern of the ship only, both of which were vertical and about 50 feet clear of the water. There was very little wreckage. The six survivors were supported by a target raft and floating timber till picked up by HMS Badger shortly after 7 p.m. Only one man besides those rescued was seen to come to the surface after the explosion, and he sank before he could reach the target raft.*" [75]

In writing about his death a week later, The Rossendale Free Press reported that Tom's mother had received a letter from the Admiralty informing her that her son's ship had been sunk by the enemy on 31st May 1916 and that, "*in the absence of his name appearing on the list of survivors, he must be presumed to have lost his life in the sinking.*"

Eighteen when he died, Tom had been home on leave the previous month and was reported to have been very cheerful.[76] His name is engraved on the Plymouth Naval

---

[75] dreadnoughtproject.org - Report of Commander H Dannreuther, Gun Control Officer
[76] Rossendale Free Press 10th June 1916

Memorial[77] which overlooks Plymouth Sound. The memorial was built after the war as a means of commemorating all those naval personnel who had lost their lives during the conflict and whose only grave was the sea. Identical monuments were raised at Portsmouth and Chatham, the other two main naval ports that had seen ships go off to war.

In Rawtenstall, Tom Fielding is remembered on the town's war memorial in the local cemetery and at St Mary's Church, Rawtenstall. The church is only a few hundred yards from the house in St Mary's Place where Tom and his siblings grew up.

Plymouth Naval Memorial and Inscription

---

[77] Memorial Photographs: The War Graves Photographic Project

Private Frank Hitchen
Royal Marine Light Infantry
Died 25th January 1917

Remembered
Chatham Naval Memorial

Frank Hitchen[78] was born in Stacksteads on 9th July 1898, the first child born to Frank and Annie Hitchen. Following a spell working in a cotton mill, Frank's father began work as a railway porter at Accrington station and the family moved to 15 Bridge House in the town. The 1911 census confirms that at a later date and no longer employed by the railway company, Frank moved his growing family[79] back to Stacksteads and returned to work in a local cotton mill. It is possible that young Frank started school in Accrington, but it is not known when the family returned to Rossendale and no records survive that would confirm this to be the case. After their return to the valley, the family lived at Holts' Buildings in Stacksteads and Frank attended St Saviour's School before he joined Newchurch Grammar School from 7th September

---
[78] Photograph: Rossendale Free Press 17th February 1917
[79] Frank had six siblings, one of whom died in infancy

1910. When he completed his education he went to work as a clerk at a local quarry owned by Mr Henry Heys.

The Ancestry website holds a digital copy of Frank's naval service record. At the age of 17, he enlisted in the Royal Marine Light Infantry (RMLI), joining at Manchester on 23rd September 1915. Traditionally, the role of the RMLI was that of infantry who were deployed as security on board naval vessels. They also manned the gun turrets at the aft of battleships and cruisers

Frank did not enlist for the duration of the war. His record shows that he signed up for twelve years and was issued with service number CH/20234.[80] Sent to the recruitment depot in Deal for basic training, he was transferred to the naval base at Chatham on 6th April 1916. While there, he underwent gunnery and musketry training and was adjudged to be a very good infantryman, with his commanding officer writing of his very good character.[81]

Unlike the Army, the Navy was legally allowed to accept under age volunteers but these "boy sailors" were not allowed to go into combat until they were 18. When Frank reached this milestone on 15th October 1916, he joined the crew of SS *Laurentic*. Built as an ocean liner for White Star Line in 1908, the ship had previously operated on the Liverpool to Canada service. In port at Montreal when the war began, she was immediately commissioned for war service and underwent conversion to an armed cruiser. Her powerful engines meant she could outrun any German submarine of the day. She was initially used to bring Canadian troops across the Atlantic and to transport much needed raw materials and German prisoners of war from West Africa.[82]

---

[80] The CH indicates that he was based at Chatham
[81] Service Record accessed through Ancestry
[82] In 1915, forces from the Union of South Africa invaded German South West Africa on behalf of the British Imperial Government

In early 1917, the *Laurentic* was on her way to Halifax, Nova Scotia. She had left Liverpool on 23rd January but had called in at the naval base of Buncrana in the north of Ireland two days later, in order to disembark five seamen who were ill. With the five crewmen safely ashore, *Laurentic* left her berth in the middle of a heavy snow storm at 5pm on 25th January and headed out into the Atlantic Ocean. Some two miles off the coast, the ship hit a German mine and began to settle in the water. As the captain was giving the order to abandon ship she hit a second mine. This one ripped through her engine room and destroyed the generators. As a result, the pumps could no longer be deployed. Taking on water more and more rapidly, the ship sank within an hour. Eighteen year old Frank did not survive the sinking.

Only 121 of the 475 men aboard survived. Many of those who reached the lifeboats were badly injured and were exposed to low temperatures and severe wind chill. Rescue craft were delayed by the terrible weather and, when they eventually reached the lifeboats, they found many who had survived the initial sinking had died from exposure while waiting to be rescued. Around 70 bodies were recovered from both the lifeboats and from along the shoreline and they were buried in a mass grave in the churchyard at Fahan, Co Donegal.

In addition to her crew, the ship was secretly carrying around 43 tons of gold ingots valued at £5m (£388m today), in payment for munitions. Between 1917 and 1924, Royal Navy divers made over 5,000 dives to the wreck and recovered all but 22 of the ingots. These still lie on the sea bed, most likely under the ship, but remain undisturbed since the *Laurentic* is now preserved as a war grave.

Frank is remembered on the Chatham Naval Memorial[83] in Kent and on Bacup's War Memorial.[84] After his death, friends and family described him as "*a regular and clever scholar of quiet disposition who had won a number of scholarships*" and "*a most promising and exemplary young man of fine character and attainments and [that] a career of honour and usefulness was predicted for him.*" [85]

Chatham Naval Memorial

---

[83] Memorial Photograph: The War Graves Photographic Project
[84] Now installed at the ABC Centre, Burnley Rd, Bacup
[85] Bacup Times: 3rd February 1917

Chapter 6

The last attack of the Somme Offensive, the Battle of the Ancre, was called off on 18th November 1916. Over the four and a half months from 1st July, the allies had only advanced 6 miles, despite having launched around 90 separate attacks. Following the onset of bad weather, Haig put operations in the area on hold until spring. During the Somme campaign the British had suffered 420,000 casualties, 125,000 of whom had been killed.

The cold, wet winter weather set in towards the end of October and ground conditions on the Somme deteriorated rapidly. Both armies dug in to their positions and prepared to spend one of the harshest winters of the war out in the open. As the heavy rain continued unabated, the trenches became waterlogged and muddy.

The winter of 1916/17 saw temperatures regularly fall below zero. There was almost continuous rain, sleet, snow and frost. Even with duckboards positioned in the bottom of the trenches, men found themselves standing for hours in the mud and icy water. This often led to the development of trench foot which, if not treated quickly, could progress to gangrene. Despite soldiers' best efforts, general conditions were insanitary and disease levels rose.

With their uniforms and kit soaked and muddy, men struggled to keep warm. Even though it was bitterly cold, it was an offence to light any type of fire or brazier where trenches ran close to German lines, since this might help the enemy to direct their artillery onto British positons. In an effort to find some warmth and shelter from the elements, soldiers often attempted to dig holes into the trench sides but the ground was frozen so deeply that they were unable to scrape out more than a shallow hollow.

Although there was very little activity on either side during the winter months, preparations were being made for their resumption in spring. The allies were planning two offensives. The first, in early March, would attempt to capture the German-held ridge near the river Ancre that overlooked British lines on the northern flank of the Somme battlefield. The second was to be an attack on German lines in an area to the east of the town of Arras.

Four of the former Newchurch Grammar School pupils were killed during these attacks; one died on the Somme and three at Arras. All of them are among the missing.

Private Wilfred Crowther
2nd Battalion, East Lancashire Regiment
Died 4th March 1917

Remembered
Thiepval Memorial

Wilfred Crowther[86] was born in Waterfoot on 14th February 1894. He lived at 683 Bacup Road in the town with his parents, Joseph and Sarah, and his elder brother and younger sister. Initially educated at Waterfoot Council School, he was admitted to Newchurch Grammar School on 8th May 1906. His father was a self-employed joiner and cabinet maker and when Wilfred finished at school he became his father's apprentice.

Wilfred's service record has not survived, and when information was sought from the CWGC database, it produced records for two men named Wilfred Crowther who had served in Lancashire Regiments and another, a W Crowther, of the Manchester Regiment. The websites

---

[86] Photograph by kind permission of Terry Heard, co-author of the website: www.WW1cemeteries.com

Soldiers Died in the Great War[87] and Forces War Records[88] provided the additional information that only one of these men had been born in Waterfoot.

Private 22274, Wilfred Crowther, enlisted at Rawtenstall and joined the 2nd Battalion, East Lancashire Regiment. Although he was 20 when war was declared and eligible to join up, no enlistment date is given on either of the two websites and no details of his military service have been found. This makes it impossible to give accurate details of where he served. It is known that the 2nd East Lancs landed at Le Havre on 6th November 1914 and saw service at the Battle of Neuve Chapelle in 1915 and in the area around the village of Contalmaison during the first Battle of the Somme. There is nothing to confirm whether Wilfred was serving with them during this period.

The National Archives' large collection of war diaries is extremely useful when researching a specific battalion and the entries can be used to produce a timeline for the period immediately before the death of a member of the battalion. The 2nd East Lancashire's diary shows that in March 1917 they were in the north west of France, in the area of the river Ancre in Picardy.[89] On the 1st of the month, a fine sunny day, all companies had enjoyed baths and foot treatments in the morning and rifle and Lewis gun inspections in the afternoon. Following a frosty night, 2nd March dawned cold and damp, and after a scheduled battalion parade in the morning, the troops moved forward into the front line trenches in the early afternoon.

The night of 2nd/3rd March was again cold and frosty. The men received orders to prepare for an imminent attack on the

---

[87] Accessed at the Find My Past website
[88] Forces War Records
[89] National Archives Ref WO95/1720/2

German-held ridge that overlooked British positions. The plans that were issued had gone into great detail and stipulated three things: to be less conspicuous to enemy snipers and machine gunners, officers were to dress in the same uniforms as their men; precautions were to be taken to stop any machine gun barrages falling on friendly troops; observers' positions and the calculation of distances to be relayed to the artillery were to be made with the greatest care. All three were issues that had blighted previous attacks.

The diary details what happened in the attack.[90] Due to the freezing weather, troops were unable to dig their pre-planned assembly trenches, with the result that the leading waves had to form up out in the open, on lines of white tape laid out to represent the trenches. The battalion advanced at 5.15am. In his report back to headquarters, the Captain of Wilfred's Company, Captain P Bellamy, said that his troops were moving forward although they were having "a rough time" as the enemy artillery was very active.[91] Heavy enemy shelling continued throughout the night of $4^{th}/5^{th}$ March, and the troops' situation was not made any easier by a heavy fall of snow. The following morning, the number of casualties was confirmed as 4 officers wounded, 11 other ranks killed and 39 wounded. In addition, a number of men were listed as missing and, according to the war diary, Pte Crowther of 5 Platoon, B Company was one of those who failed to return.

Some of the missing soldiers returned to their battalion the day after the attack. In the confusion of the aftermath of the attack, they had lost their bearings and had been unable to find their way back to their trench. A search patrol was later sent out to look for the remaining missing men. There is nothing in the diary to say if anyone else was brought back to the lines but 23-year-old Wilfred Crowther was never found.

---

[90] National Archives Ref WO95/1720/2
[91] Ibid

Within the pages of the diary is a hand written report of the attack, written by Captain Bellamy. *"I must say that my company has had a rougher time than I expected."*[92] He finished by criticising the way in which his section commanders had led their men, despite the fact that everyone had received clear instructions before the attack commenced.

Wilfred Crowther was one of nearly 20,000 officers and men of the East Lancashire Regiment who died in the Great War. His name is engraved on Pier 6, Face C of the Thiepval Memorial with others of his regiment who have no known grave. He was also remembered on the WW1 memorial stained glass window installed after the war in Waterfoot's Bethlehem Unitarian Church. The church was demolished in 1987 and it appears that the memorial was lost at that time.

Inscription from the Thiepval Memorial

---

[92] National Archives Ref WO95/1720/2
Thiepval Inscription Image: The War Graves Photographic Project

Captain Edward Martin Wright
5th Battalion, East Lancashire Regiment
Died 10th April 1917

Remembered
Arras Memorial, France

Edward Martin Wright was born on 19th November 1891. He was the youngest son of Edward Wright, a Bacup solicitor and clerk to the Rossendale Justices, and his second wife Rebecca. Edward Snr also had six children with his first wife, Mary, who died in 1885.

Edward was only 9 years old when his father died. He had been home schooled in his early years and attended Newchurch Grammar School from 1900 until 1904, at which date he transferred to Manchester Grammar School and remained a pupil there until 1910.[93] A good scholar, he gained a place at King's College Cambridge to study Law; while there

---

[93] https://sites.google.com/sites/mgsww1/

he joined the university rowing club, where he often coxed the first team and acted as a coach.[94]

Edward's half-brother Alexander (Alex) had also studied Law at Cambridge and on qualifying he had joined his father's firm. After graduation, Edward also returned to Bacup to complete his professional examinations, working beside Alex in the family firm.

Very few records relating to Edward's military service remain, but some basic information was found in newspaper archives. In reporting the news of his death in 1917, the Bacup Times noted that he had joined the colours at the start of the war.[95] The London Gazette's supplement in September 1914 announced that Edward had been commissioned into the 5th East Lancashire Regiment as a 2nd Lieutenant.[96] He was later promoted to a full lieutenant.

The Bacup Times obituary included the detail that, at the time he was killed, Edward had been attached to the 9th East Lancs with the rank of Captain. However, both the CWGC database and the Officer Long Number files at the National Archives[97] confirm that this was incorrect. He was in fact attached to the regiment's 8th battalion.

The Lancashire Evening Post's obituary reported that he went out to France in January 1917 but there was nothing in the article to indicate how he had spent the two and a half years between joining up and embarking for the front.[98] Without access to a service record, any discussion about this has to be conjecture and the following outline is merely a suggestion, based on the available facts.

---

[94] Yorkshire Post and Leeds Intelligencer: 21st April 1917
[95] Bacup Times: 21st April 1917
[96] London Gazette: 4th September 1914
[97] National Archives Ref WO 374/77093
[98] Lancashire Evening Post: 25th April 1917

Edward's Medal Index Card (MIC) is held at the National Archives and shows that he was posthumously awarded the British War and Victory Medals, although there is no record of his having received either the 1914 or 1914/15 stars. Receipt of one or other of these campaign medals would indicate that he had fought overseas at some time between 4th August 1914 and 31st December 1915. The absence of either medal suggests he remained on Home Service until at least January 1916.

Edward would have spent a number of months in training and learning the skills required to be a junior officer. By looking at the history of the 5th East Lancs Regiment, it is possible to suggest where he spent the remaining months before he went to France in 1917.

Following Lord Kitchener's call to arms, many regiments were inundated with vast numbers of volunteers and, in order to accommodate them all, additional battalions were raised.[99] In September 1914 a major part of the 5th East Lancs left for Egypt, renamed the 1/5th battalion East Lancashire Regiment; they later fought at Gallipoli and were eligible to receive the 1914/15 star for their service in the Eastern Mediterranean. With no record of his having been awarded this particular medal, it is unlikely Edward served with the battalion.

When the 1/5th went abroad, they left behind around 80 other ranks and *"two or three disappointed and unhappy officers"*.[100] These men became the nucleus of the new 2/5th battalion who began recruiting in the Blackburn and Burnley areas on 5th September. The men lived initially in their own homes and travelled to their training depots daily before they moved to Southport in November.[101] In May 1915 they moved to

---

[99] By the end of WW1, the East Lancs Regiment had raised 17 battalions
[100] History of the East Lancashire Regiment
[101] The troops received allowances for food and rail travel

Sussex and spent the summer under canvas training in field and trench craft.

By March of 1916, the battalion had moved to the Divisional Headquarters at Colchester where they became part of the East coast defences. During the time they were at Colchester, drafts of both officers and men were sent to reinforce other battalions already fighting abroad and it was not until March 1917 that the 2/5th went out to France.

There is a high probability that Edward served with the 2/5th East Lancs while they were England. The fact that he arrived in France in January 1917[102] suggests that he was sent out as part of reinforcements and that this was when he was promoted to Captain and attached to the 8th battalion, the battalion with which he was serving when he was reported missing in action.

The 8th battalion had landed in France in July 1915. At the end of 1916 they moved north, away from their positions on the Somme, and by January were out of the line and in General Headquarters Reserve. They did not return to front line duties until early February 1917, at which time Edward may have joined them. An officer writing up the war diary on their arrival noted that "*the most noticeable features on the front were the enormous number of heavy enemy trench mortars, the thickness of the enemy wire and the lack of this on our side.*"[103] In early March, they moved to the Divisional training area behind Arras where preparations were underway for a major attack. If successful, this would break through German lines and end the deadlock on the Western Front.

A huge preliminary barrage on enemy lines began on 4th April and carried on constantly over the next few days.[104]

---

[102] Lancashire Evening Post: 25th April 1917
[103] History of the East Lancashire Regiment: Vol II, page 430
[104] The barrage was heavier than the one on the first day of the Somme and more successful.

Zero hour had originally been set for 8th April but was delayed 24 hours at the request of the French. In order to reach their assembly point in the old British line west of Arras, the 8th East Lancs had to march some eighty miles in wet weather.

Edward's battalion moved forward towards their jumping off positions under considerable machine gun fire. On reaching their first objective, they found that the main attack had been held up, and this stalled their own advance. Soon after dark, as snow began to fall and it became bitterly cold, the order was given for the whole Division to dig in.

The following day, the attack was renewed and the 8th battalion moved forward under cover of a heavy snowstorm. They soon came under intense enemy rifle and machine-gun fire and lost touch with the rest of the attacking force. The official battalion history notes that *"it was around this time Captain Wright was killed."* [105] Edward's family were initially informed that he was missing in action. Some days later, his brother received official notification that the body had been found and buried by his comrades.[106] Unfortunately, the burial site was later lost due to heavy fighting in the area.

Edward is remembered on the Arras Memorial to the Missing. The Memorial commemorates nearly 35,000 soldiers from Britain, South Africa and New Zealand who were killed during the period 9th April to 16th May 1917 and who have no known grave.

He is also remembered on the Bacup War Memorial, at King's College, Cambridge and at Christ Church, Bacup. After her husband's death, Edward's mother moved to St Anne's, where her son is remembered on the war memorial.

---

[105] History of the East Lancashire Regiment: Vol II, page 433
[106] Bacup Times: 28th April 1917

Private Fred Howorth
Royal Marine Light Infantry
Died 28th April 1917

Remembered
Arras Memorial, France

Fred Howorth[107] was born at 14 Brearley Street, Stacksteads on 2nd February 1896 to Henry, a quarryman, and his wife Hannah. His early years were spent at Western School before he was enrolled at Newchurch Grammar School on 19th January 1909. By the age of 15 he had completed his education and was working as an apprentice plumber. In his spare time he was deputy organist at his local church.[108]

A search on the military history archives site Forces War Records[109] found information relating to one PO/1358(S), Fred Howorth of the Royal Marines Light Infantry (RMLI).

---

[107] Photograph: Rossendale Free Press 16th June 1917
The Honour Roll at BRGS and the Rossendale Free Press use the spelling Haworth, but Lancashire BMD, census records, Fred's naval service record, the CWGC website and Forces War Records all use Howorth. The latter spelling is used here.
[108] Probably St Saviour's Church, Bacup as Fred's name appears on the church's war memorial
[109] Forces War Records

The record shows an identical date of birth, home address and paternal forename which is sufficient to confirm the record is Fred's. The service number's two-letter prefix 'PO' signifies that he joined the Portsmouth Division of the RMLI when he enlisted. The letter 'S' after the service number denotes a short term post for the duration of the war.[110]

Before 1914, a marine's primary occupation was to supplement a ship's crew and man the guns. There was little or no opportunity for service on land. On the declaration of war, having filled all available ship vacancies, the Navy was faced with a surplus of some 20,000 marine reserves. In order to accommodate these supernumeraries, three new brigades were raised, two naval and one marine, with the latter to be purely a land-based operational unit.

By 1916, the Marine Brigade had fought in land battles in France, Egypt, Gallipoli and Salonica and with little prospect of being called to action at sea, the decision was made to transfer it from the authority of the Admiralty to that of the War Office. The Marine Brigade joined the British Army, as part of the 63rd (Royal Naval) Division on 29th April and left the eastern Mediterranean bound for France in May 1916. Having landed at Marseilles, the marines gradually moved northwards and arrived on the Western Front in time to take part in the final phase of the Battle of the Somme (the Battle of the River Ancre) in November 1916.

Fred Howorth's Certificate of Service is held at the National Archives.[111] This shows that he enlisted at Manchester on 17th January 1916 and was sent to the Royal Marine Recruitment Depot at Deal. From 30th March to 27th June he was stationed in barracks at Portsmouth Dockyard before he was posted to HMS *Victory*, Portsmouth's shore-based station. On 2nd February 1917 he embarked for France

---

[110] nmrn.org.uk/research/service-record-abbreviations
[111] National Archives Ref ADM 159/205/1358

and joined the 2nd Battalion, Royal Marine Light Infantry (RMLI), part of the Marine Brigade.

The 1917 battalion war diary illustrates what life at the front would have been like for Fred and his comrades. The battalion had been heavily involved in operations along the Ancre since January and when February ushered in a period of intense frost that lasted for days, trench life became even more difficult. Relieved from front line duties on 8th of February, troops retired to huts at Martinsart, a small village to the north of Albert. This was short respite, as they returned to the trenches a few days later with orders to consolidate their positions along a line of shell holes. Here the battalion remained until 22nd February when they were rewarded with a well-earned period of rest behind the lines.[112]

In early March, Fred's battalion moved to Bouzincourt, north-west of Albert. Formed into working parties, they spent their time repairing roads and building ammunition dumps. On 19th March, orders were received to move north and, over the next nine days and with only one day's rest, the battalion marched with full kit and equipment over 75 miles from Rubempré, near Albert to Fouquières, east of Lens. The route was over rough and difficult terrain and on arriving at their destination the men were given no time to rest before they assumed their new positions. The last days of February were taken up with numerous training exercises in preparation for the forthcoming Arras Offensive.

Although the Battle of Arras began on 9th April, the war diary confirms that the 2nd battalion were not immediately deployed. For most of the month they were involved in training exercises and working parties and only went into the attack on 25th April when they moved into newly captured trenches in the village of Gavrelle.

---

[112] Nat Archives Ref WO95/3110/2

On 28th April, both the 1st and 2nd battalions RMLI took part in a Divisional attack on German defensive lines on the edge of the village.[113] The plan was for the 2nd battalion to capture the village windmill, located on higher ground and with a good view of the plain below, before pushing forward to take a line of unfinished German trenches where they were to dig in. Zero hour was at 4.25am and, having successfully taken the windmill, the 2nd RMLI moved on to their next objective. They were to be supported in this action by the 1st battalion after they had achieved their own first objective, but their initial attack had been a total disaster and the 1st Battalion was almost completely wiped out. Even without the expected assistance of the 1st RMLI, the 2nd battalion succeeded in taking both their targets but they were unable to hold the ground against a very strong German counter attack. Almost immediately after they had entered the German frontline trenches, a heavy enemy artillery attack blasted them out again. Those who survived were cut off but fought on, incurring many casualties. A brave few made their way back to their own lines, while others were taken prisoner.

The 28th April attack, the Battle of Gavrell, saw the highest number of marine casualties in any one day in the history of the corps.[114] In total, 846 marines were listed as killed, missing or wounded. The 2nd battalion's casualties amounted to one officer and one other rank killed and 8 officers and 387 other ranks missing. One of the missing was Fred, whose body was never found. He is remembered with others of his regiment on the Arras Memorial. His name is also included on the war memorial in St Saviour's Church, Bacup

---

[114] www.royalmarinehistory.com/post/the-battle-of-gavrell-windmill

2nd Lieutenant John Elwyn Slater
5th East Lancashire Regiment
Died 3rd May 1917

Remembered
Arras Memorial, France

John Elwyn Slater[115] was the second eldest of three children born to George Slater and his wife Annie. At the time of his birth on 29th June 1890, John's father was the manager of a local cotton mill and the family were living at 6 Princess Street in Haslingden. They later moved to 2 Wells Street before settling at Belgrave House. After his father retired, the family moved to Lytham.

John began his education at Commercial Primary, Haslingden, followed by a period at Haslingden Secondary School before he was admitted to Newchurch Grammar School on 14th January 1904. He was also a boarder at Western College in Harrogate for a time although it is not clear whether this was before or after he attended NGS. By the date of the 1911 census, John had finished school and was working as a clerk in a cotton mill. There is nothing to confirm whether this was the same factory as that in which

---

[115] Photograph: Haslingden Guardian

his father worked. He was later promoted to assistant manager and company secretary. On 7th October 1916 he married Margaret Fielding, a 24-year-old local junior school teacher.

The National Archives holds a file for John which confirms that he joined up on 7th December 1915. This was just before conscription was introduced by the Military Service Bill in January 1916. His Medal Index card is also stored at Kew and shows that he originally joined the army as a Private and was posted to the 2/28th Battalion, London Regiment (Artists Rifles) with the service number 5873.

In October 1914, the Artists' Rifles Battalion[116] had become an Officer Training Corps. Men posted to this battalion had been selected as prospective officers and, on completion of their training, were transferred to other units. After a period of basic training, John went as an officer cadet to Hare Hall Camp in Havering, East London. He received his commission on 11th July 1916[117] and was posted to the 5th Battalion, East Lancashire Regiment as a probationary 2nd Lieutenant. By May 1917, John was attached to the 2nd battalion, Lancashire Fusiliers, although there is nothing to confirm when this occurred.

The action in which John Slater died is now known as the Third Battle of the Scarpe, one of many phases in the Battle of Arras which was fought between 9th April and 17th June 1917. The town had become a German stronghold and the allied plan of attack was drawn up in the hope of making a strategic breakthrough and ending the stalemate that had developed in Northern France. It was also aimed at diverting German attention away from the French, who had run into difficulties while attacking along the river Aisne. Notable for

---

[116] Over 15,000 men joined the Artists' Rifles during the war, 10,000 of whom became officers.
[117] Supplement to London Gazette: 24 July 1916

the spectacular gains made by the allies in the first two days, the Battle of Arras faltered after the Germans brought up their reserves and counter-attacked. While the allies continued to make some small gains, rising casualty figures and the lack of any real forward progress eventually resulted in abandonment of the offensive.

At 3.45am on 3rd May, as part of the allied offensive that was to take place over a 21km front, the 2nd Lancashire Fusiliers moved forward into an attack that is recognised today as one of the darkest days of the war. It began to go wrong from the very beginning. Due to the early morning darkness, many units were unable to find their starting point and there was confusion as to the direction in which they should be going. The 2nd battalion's war diary details what happened to them that day. In position to the north-east of Arras, the unit's four companies left their trenches at zero hour, under a covering barrage. The route of the attack was up a railway embankment but, due to its height and the darkness, two of the battalion's four companies were unable to keep up with the others. This resulted in the other two companies going forward as planned, but with no cover on either flank. The battalion diary notes that "no one of these two companies who went through has since returned."[118]

The attack was summed up in the official history of war operations and gave the following reasons for the failure. *"The confusion caused by the darkness; the speed with which the German artillery opened fire; the manner in which it concentrated upon the British infantry, almost neglecting the artillery; the intensity of its fire, the heaviest that many an experienced soldier had ever witnessed, seemingly unchecked by British counter-battery fire and lasting almost without slackening for fifteen hours; the readiness with which the German infantry yielded to the first assault and the energy of its counter-*

---

[118] National Archives Ref WO95/1507-2

attack; and, it must be added, the bewilderment of the British infantry on finding itself in the open and its inability to withstand any resolute counter-attack."[119] It is also notable that General Haig had his own concerns. In his diary for 2nd May, he wrote of his misgivings about the attack that was planned for early the next morning. He was well aware of the German artillery's strong response to previous staggered attacks by the Australians and British, but despite this he let the attack go ahead, with disastrous results. The war diary for 3rd May lists 2nd Lieutenant J E Slater as "wounded and missing."[120] John was 27 years old and was one of the battalion's 14 officers and 275 other ranks killed, wounded or listed as missing that day.

It was only on 2nd August 1919 that the war office confirmed his death officially. In view of the length of time that had elapsed and in the absence of his name on any German list of prisoners, he was considered to have been killed on or after 3rd May 1917. His name is on the Arras Memorial. He is also remembered on the Haslingden Municipal War Memorial and at St James the Great Church.

St James' Memorial[121]

---

[119] The Official History: Military Operations France and Belgium 1917 Volume 1 by Captain Cyril Falls. Naval & Military Press 2013
[120] National Archives Ref WO 95/1507/1
[121] Picture courtesy of St James the Great Church Haslingden

Chapter 7

The defences on the Western Front stretched from the Swiss border to the North Sea, a distance of 440 miles. French troops were concentrated in the southern section of the line, with British and colonial troops occupying the area from the Somme, through the Ypres salient and up to the coast. Despite heavy fighting in Flanders during 1914 and 1915, little had changed along the front. The Allies still held the land around the now ruined city of Ypres but their position was surrounded on three sides by an enemy who held most of the high ground overlooking British lines. By 1916, consideration was being given to a plan to oust the Germans from their position on the Messines Ridge but this was postponed as allied efforts were concentrated further south on the Somme and at Verdun.

With the Somme offensive having failed to make the expected breakthrough, Haig turned his attention back to Flanders and in particular to the Messines Ridge. If it could be captured, it would provide access for an advance on the Passchendaele Ridge and from there, northwards to the coast. Controlling the coast up to the Dutch border would deny the enemy access to coastal supply routes and increase supply options for the allies. It would also avoid any possibility of a seaborne attack on the British mainland.

Although the main allied focus in 1916 had been further south in France, since 1915 British tunnelling companies in Flanders had been digging out a vast network of mineshafts about 40 metres under No Man's Land. These tunnels led towards, and eventually underneath, German positions on the Messines Ridge. A large cavern was dug at the end of each shaft and then packed with huge quantities of explosive. By early 1917 a total of twenty-one mines had been completed, stretching under the entire length of the ridge.

As the British excavated their shafts, the Germans were digging their own tunnels towards them. Both sides placed officers with stethoscopes deep in the tunnels, listening for any sound of the enemy nearby. If anything was heard, explosives were detonated and the resultant cave-in killed or trapped the enemy underground.

Before the attack on Messines Ridge began on 7th June, a preliminary bombardment continued day and night throughout most of May. It steadily increased in intensity before it ceased exactly half an hour before dawn on the day of the attack. At precisely ten past three, nineteen of the twenty-one mines were blown,[122] instantly killing around 10,000 enemy troops who were occupying the ridge. A massive artillery barrage followed before some 9 allied divisions, each of between 12,000 and 14,000 men, went into the attack.

Messines Ridge was in British hands by 9am. It had been captured with a far lower casualty rate than expected, but as victorious allied soldiers surged forward during the morning, the ridge became overcrowded and troops were easily picked off by German gunners positioned on the opposite slope. The enemy counter-attacked around 11am, but a British artillery barrage, coupled with intense machine gun fire, ensured its failure. The Germans continued to counter-attack over the following days. With each attempt they lost further ground, and by the time the attack was called off on 14th June, the entire Messines salient was in British hands.

---

[122] One tunnel had collapsed while being prepared and the primed mine still lies 80 feet below the surface in the area of Douve Farm. A second was abandoned following German mining activity in the area which smashed the galleries and severed the detonation leads to the mine. An attempt to rewire it ran out of time.

Private Ronald Andrew
11th Battalion, Cheshire Regiment
Died 13th June 1917

Remembered
The Menin Gate Memorial

Ronald Andrew,[123] son of Edwin and Margaret Andrew, was born in Waterfoot on 22nd August 1897. The family lived at 41 Burnley Road, from where Edwin ran his butchery business. Ronald first attended Primary School in Waterfoot before he was admitted on a scholarship to Newchurch Grammar School on 7th September 1910.

When he finished his education, he joined the staff of the Manchester & County Bank and completed the Institute of Bankers examinations. The Manchester & County Bank later became part of what is now NatWest Group. For the centenary of the Great War, the Group[124] created a website to honour the 1,582 members of staff who fell in the conflict. The notes for Ronald indicate that he joined the bank in October 1913 and was working as a clerk at the Waterfoot branch when war broke out. A scholar at Bethesda United

---

[123] Photograph reproduced by kind permission of NatWest Group © 2021
[124] At that date known as the Royal Bank of Scotland Group

Methodist Sunday School and a member of the Young Men's Class, he was known to be of a kindly disposition and much loved by all who knew him.[125]

Ronald's army record still survives at the National Archives in Kew. He enlisted at Rawtenstall on 7th June 1916, two months short of his nineteenth birthday,[126] and was posted to the Reserves while he waited to be called up to his regiment. Due to the large number of recruits that had to be processed, this took over three months. As Private 32692, he joined the 3rd battalion of the King's Shropshire Light Infantry (KSLI) on 3rd October 1916.

On 27th February 1917, he left Southampton as part of the British Expeditionary Force (BEF) and made his way to the Infantry Base Depots at Rouen.[127] This was a major collection point for troops heading to the Western Front. Initially attached to the 7th battalion KSLI, he was posted to the 11th Battalion, Cheshire Regiment on 22nd March and issued with the new service number 50712.[128] Wounded in action on 30th May, his service record shows that he was back in the trenches by early June. The final entry simply states that he was killed in action on 13th June 1917. There is nothing in the file to indicate where or how he died. He was 19 years old and had been serving for nine months.

The 11th Cheshire battalion's war diary for June 1917 provides information about the days leading up to Ronald's death.[129] They were in Flanders, working under the instruction of the 130th Field Company, Royal Engineers and

---

[125] Rossendale Free Press: 30th June, 1917
[126] The 1916 Military Services Act had set the lower age limit for conscription at 19 but this was amended to 18 on 25th May 1916.
[127] Rouen lay safely behind the lines and was the location for several base hospitals and infantry depots. From August 1916, Infantry Base Depots were responsible for supplying drafts to regiments.
[128] Service Record at Ancestry
[129] National Archives Ref 95/2250/1

were engaged in improving assembly trenches and overland tracks just behind the front line. Although the men were unaware of the reason, the work was being carried out in preparation for the planned attack on the Messines Ridge. The nature of the work and its proximity to the front line meant that everything had to be done at night.

When the attack on the ridge began, the 11th Cheshire regiment were in Reserve as part of the 75th Brigade. They were heavily shelled while waiting in the assembly trenches but suffered few casualties after they moved forward into the attack. After the successful capture of the ridge, the battalion remained in the line until they were relieved on 9th June when they returned to their camp behind the lines. They moved back into the front line to the east of Messines during the night of 12th/13th June and at 7.30pm on the 13th, the enemy opened up a very heavy bombardment which lasted about ninety minutes. When it came to an end, 32 other ranks had been killed. Although he was not mentioned by name, it is possible that Ronald was one of the casualties that night.

In reporting his death, the Rossendale Free Press[130] wrote that *"No official information of this sad occurrence has yet been received but the news has been conveyed to the parents in letters from a lieutenant and a corporal of the company to which Pte Andrews was attached."* The report also quoted from a letter from Ronald's commanding officer to his parents. *"I can remember when your boy joined this battalion which has done such magnificent work in the last great battle.[131] Since his arrival out here I have been interested in his welfare, one reason being because he was quite an educated lad. At the beginning of this month he suffered a slight injury to his eye which necessitated his going into hospital. He returned, I believe, on the 11th inst looking very happy and cheery. Two days later he met his death".*

---

[130] Rossendale Free Press: June 30th, 1917
[131] The attack on Messines Ridge

A comrade who had trained with him said he had lost "*a good friend who would do no-one any harm. . . . . and who would be much missed by all the platoon.*"[132] The newspaper article concluded by reporting that "*The deceased soldier was a young man of considerable promise and had the war not intervened would undoubtedly have made considerable headway in civil life.*"[133]

Ronald is one of over 54,000 men remembered on the Menin Gate. The memorial was erected on the site of the gateway through which hundreds of thousands of allied servicemen marched on their way to the battlefields of Flanders. After his death he was remembered on the Bethesda United Methodist Church war memorial in Waterfoot. Since the church's closure and later demolition, the plaque has been installed at Newchurch Methodist Church, Turnpike.

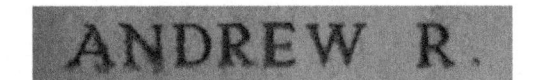

Menin Gate Inscription

---

[132] Rossendale Free Press: June 30th, 1917
[133] Ibid

Gunner Joseph Harvey
Royal Field Artillery
Died 12th July 1917

Dozinghem Military Cemetery
Near Poperinghe, Belgium

Joseph Harvey,[134] the second child of Joseph Garibaldi Harvey and his wife Elizabeth Ann, was born in Oldham on 9th January 1896. Mr Harvey was employed as an insurance agent and this probably explains the large number of house moves undertaken by the family. Joseph's father was later promoted to the post of Assurance Superintendent and the 1911 census shows that in the years after Joseph's birth, five further children had been born to the couple.

When the family moved to Bacup, young Joseph attended Mount School before he progressed to Newchurch Grammar School in 1908. By 1911 he had completed his education and was working as a grocer's assistant. When the family moved

---

[134] Photograph: Blackpool Herald 20 July 1917

to Blackpool, Joseph began work at the bottling stores of Catterall and Swarbrick's Brewery on Central Drive[135].

Although the CWGC database is often the first place to look for information relating to war casualties, a search for 'Joseph Harvey' brought up 177 results. With such a large number of results from the CWGC, other records had to be interrogated in an effort to find information about Joseph's war service. A search of the 'Register of Soldiers' Effects'[136] found an entry for Gunner 680295, Joseph Harvey of the Royal Field Artillery (RFA). This entry listed the relatives among whom the soldier's effects had been shared and the names matched those of Joseph's family as detailed in the 1911 census.

Gunner Harvey's Medal Index Card (MIC) at the National Archives holds some basic information.[137] Assigned to the RFA as a driver, he went out to France on 30th Sept 1915. He was issued, firstly, with the service number 1367 and then with 680295. A four figure service number superseded by a six figure one indicates that the soldier was originally a member of the Territorial Force. Confident that the correct person had been identified, a further search of the CWGC database was made. This time the search provided the information that Joseph had served in A battery of the 276th Brigade, RFA.

Until 15th May 1916, the 276th Brigade RFA was known as the 1/2nd West Lancashire Brigade. It was created specifically for the new Territorial Force that had been created under the Haldane Army Reforms of 1908. Mobilised on 4/5th August 1914, the Brigade underwent a long period of training before they left for the Front armed with 18 pounder howitzers.

---

[135] Blackpool Times: 18th July 1917
[136] A government publication issued in 1921, now held at the Army Museum and accessible online at Ancestry
[137] National Archives Ref WO 372/9/71845

These artillery pieces fired heavy shells in a curved trajectory and were used to best effect against fortifications.

The Brigade landed in France on 1st October 1915 as the divisional artillery for the 55th (West Lancashire) Division. After action near Arras, they moved south and during the Battle of the Somme, were tasked with capturing the village of Guillemont and nearby German trenches. After taking part in the battles of Guillemont and Ginchy, they received orders to move up to the Flanders area of Belgium in late September 1916 and took up position at Ypres.

Joseph's service record has not survived, but the Register of Soldiers' Effects indicates that he died on 12th July 1917 at 4th Casualty Clearing Station (CCS). In July 1917, groups of CCSs had been placed at three locations near the Flanders town of Poperinghe, in readiness for the planned offensive on the Salient.[138] The troops jokingly called these units Bandaghem, Mendinghem and Dozinghem. The last of these was the location of No 4 CCS.

By reading the unit war diary for the months leading up to Joseph's death, it can be seen that the brigade's artillery batteries were not only heavily involved in firing on the enemy's trenches but also on their forward defences, in an attempt to remove any obstacles to an allied advance. Towards the end of June 1916 the ferocity of German shelling on allied lines increased substantially and the batteries of the 276th Brigade were continuously sending over retaliatory fire.

Unfortunately, the entries for the months of July to September 1917 are missing from the Brigade War Diary held at the National Archives. This means there is no way of knowing what action Joseph was involved in that would have led to his being admitted to the medical unit. Nor is there

---

[138] Third Battle of Ypres began 31st July and continued until 10th Nov

anything to indicate how long he was treated there before he died. He was buried in Dozinghem Military Cemetery and lies in Plot I.C.9.

Although he had lived in Rossendale and was educated at NGS, Joseph is not remembered locally other than on the BRGS Roll of Honour. Having moved to live and work in Blackpool, he is remembered on the town's war memorial which stands on Central Promenade. Reports of his death were carried in The Blackpool Times, the Blackpool Herald and the Gazette News.[139] No reports of his death were found in any of the Rossendale newspaper archives.

Dozinghem Military Cemetery

Joseph Harvey's Headstone

---

[139] 18th, 20th and 24th July 1917 respectively

Chapter 8

The 1916 Battle of Jutland was the only major sea battle of World War I. It remains one of the biggest in naval history, although the result was inconclusive, with both sides claiming victory. Britain lost more ships and her casualties were almost double those of the enemy. The majority of the German fleet fled back to their base unscathed, but Britain retained control of the seas and maintained her naval blockade, barring access to the North Sea and the English Channel. Germany never again confronted British naval power in a full scale battle, and for the remainder of the war she concentrated on submarine attacks.

Both the British and German navies made use of submarines in the First World War. When Britain began her blockade of the North Sea, Germany's U-boats retaliated by sinking merchant ships that were bringing supplies across the Atlantic. Initially, U-boat captains had surfaced and given ships warning before they attacked, allowing time for crew and passengers to enter the lifeboats. After Britain began arming her merchant ships in 1915, Germany declared the seas around Britain a war zone and began a campaign of unrestricted submarine warfare, firing without warning and declaring she would sink merchant vessels from all nations found sailing in British waters. When this action culminated in the sinking of the British passenger liner Lusitania in May 1915, with the deaths of 1201 people, 128 of them American, President Woodrow Wilson sent a letter demanding Germany desist from attacking unarmed merchant ship. Fearing that America might enter the war on the side of the allies, the German government brought in new rules of engagement, but the German Navy deemed these to be so restrictive that they had stopped all U-boat attacks by September 1915.

By late 1916, with no apparent end to the stalemate on the Western Front in sight, German naval commanders began pressing for the reintroduction of unrestricted submarine warfare. They were convinced that, by attacking supply ships in British waters, they would secure a stranglehold on the allied war effort and so bring the war to an end. Having convinced the Kaiser and his government of the importance of this strategy, submarine attacks recommenced on 1st February 1917. As a direct result of this decision, two former pupils serving on British ships were killed in separate incidents when their vessels were torpedoed by German submarines.

Royal Navy Battleship firing a broadside[140]

---

[140] By kind permission of The Keasbury-Gordon Photograph Archive

Assistant Paymaster Frank Horrocks
Royal Naval Reserve
Died 15th July 1917

Naval Memorial
Plymouth

Frank Horrocks was born in Tottington, Lancashire on 8th September 1892. His father Jephthah was a calico print machinist who set up home there with his wife, Alice. The couple had six children - four daughters and two sons - of whom Frank was the third youngest. After moving to Stalybridge for a few years, the family returned to Lancashire to live at 5 Cooper Street in Bacup.

Frank attended Bacup Central Council School before he joined Newchurch Grammar School on 14th January 1904. By 1911, he had finished his formal education and was working as an articled clerk to J H Lord, a Bacup accountant. By the time he joined up in 1915, he had passed his final accountancy exams and was an Incorporated Accountant. In his spare time he was a member of the Bacup Natural History Society and attended Christ Church in Bacup.

Frank was 21 years old when the Great War began. He joined the Royal Naval Reserve on 20th March 1915 and proceeded to Portsmouth.[141] His Royal Naval Reserve service record is available on the Forces War Records website and this shows that he joined HMS *Victory*, the accounting base at Portsmouth, before he was assigned to HMS *Dreadnought* as an Assistant Paymaster on 10th April 1915. His commanding officer noted at that time that he was '*above average, accurate and painstaking.*'[142]

His work ethic and civilian training as an accountant appears to have stood him in good stead. On 29th December 1916 Frank was assigned as Temporary Assistant Paymaster in Charge on HMS *Redbreast*.[143] His commanding officer on *Dreadnought* wrote that Frank had proved himself to be '*above average, zealous, painstaking and capable*' in carrying out his duties as Captain's clerk and that he considered him suitable and competent to take up his new post.[144]

The Ancestry website holds copies of the Navy Lists. There are monthly registers of commissioned and warrant officers serving in the Royal Navy. Frank's name appears for the last time in August 1917, in a record of deceased officers who have been removed from the Navy List. He had been killed on 15th July 1917.

The new ship he had joined, SS *Redbreast*, was built in Glasgow as a passenger/cargo ship and was launched in 1908. She was requisitioned by the Admiralty in July 1915 to augment the ships of the Royal Fleet Auxiliary and, as HMS *Redbreast*, served as a Fleet Messenger in the Mediterranean. Fleet messengers varied as to type but were usually ex merchantmen and worked as regular ferries, transporting

---

[141] Bacup Times: 27 July 1917
[142] Forces War Records
[143] Temporary was used to indicate service was for the duration of the war
[144] Forces War Records

naval officers and crew to and from their naval operations. At times they had to travel through submarine zones and often had to fight their way to their destinations.

Between 20th March and 16th September 1916, *Redbreast* was reassigned for use as a 'Q-Ship', one of a series of heavily armed decoy vessels with concealed weaponry. The purpose of these vessels was to appear to be a soft target and so lure submarines into surfacing to attack, at which point the Q-ship would open fire in the hope of sinking the submarine. In mid-September 1916 she was returned to duty as a fleet messenger covering the Eastern Mediterranean.

On 15th July 1917, while on a passage between Skyros and the Doro Channel in the Aegean, *Redbreast* was torpedoed and sunk by the German mine-laying coastal submarine UC38. Forty-two members of her crew were killed, among them Frank Horrocks. He is remembered on Panel 23 of the Plymouth Naval Memorial and at Christ Church in Bacup.

In announcing Frank's death, The Bacup Times wrote that he was "*altogether a very promising young fellow, with every prospect of a bright career in front of him.*" [145]

Inscription on Plymouth Naval War Memorial

---

[145] Bacup Times: 27th July 1917

W/Op Lionel Norman Shepherd
Royal Naval Volunteer Reserve
Died 2nd July 1918

North Front Cemetery
Gibraltar

Lionel Norman Shepherd was born in Bath on 8th June 1900 and was the son of George and Leila Shepherd.[146] His early life was unsettled because his parents moved around the country looking for work. His father had been born in Sheffield and qualified as a solicitor. By 1891 he was living in London and was working part time as a singer whilst continuing in the legal profession. Census records show that George eventually gave up his legal career and became a professional singer, but in later years he was employed as an itinerant hotel-keeper. Living in Bath when Norman was

---

[146] Since his name is inscribed on the Roll of Honour as L Norman Shepherd, that format has been used in this account.
Headstone photograph: The War Graves Photographic Project

born, the family moved to Redditch and then Clevedon where George and Leila managed the Pier Hotel.

Continuing their nomadic lifestyle, the family moved north sometime in the early years of the twentieth century, although they never seemed to settle in one place for any length of time. As a consequence, Norman's education was interrupted as he moved from school to school. The family spent time in Aberdeen, where Norman attended Aberdeen Grammar School before they moved back to England.[147] He was educated at Bolton Church Institute School from January 1911 until February 1912, while his parents were manager and manageress of the Swan Hotel in Bolton.[148] He later attended Haslingden Commercial School and Mr Tattersall's private school in Haslingden[149] before he arrived at BRGS on 8th September 1914 when his father became the landlord of the Queen's Arms in Rawtenstall. Philip Clark's notes indicate that Norman's father removed him from BRGS after only a couple of terms, when he relocated to Catford, South London.[150]

A search at Ancestry found a naval service record for a Lionel Norman Shepherd. This sailor had been issued with service number Z6616 and had joined the Royal Navy Volunteer Reserve (RNVR) in May 1917. His date of birth was noted to be 27th April 1899.[151] The grammar school admission record indicate that Norman was born in June of the following year and with other genealogical databases confirming this was his birthdate, the naval record was initially dismissed. Further online searches discovered more Admiralty records and in one of these, sailor Z6616's next of

---

[147] bolton-church-institute.org.uk
[148] Ibid
[149] Rossendale Free Press: 13 July 1918
[150] Philip Lane Clark – Papers relating to BRGS Roll of Honour
[151] Ancestry

kin were given as George and Leila Shepherd.[152] This information proved that the original service record was the correct one. It appears Norman may have amended his date of birth in order to go to sea as sailors could only be sent into combat when they reached the age of eighteen.

The record gives details of Norman's training prior to going to sea. His service number was amended to LZ6616, indicating that he was in the London Division of the RNVR. There are also written comments from his superiors that show he was considered to be of very good character and carried out his duties satisfactorily.[153]

He began his life in the navy as an able seaman and trained at Victory VI, a WW1 land-based training establishment based at Crystal Palace in London. A two-month signals course followed at Vivid III and by February 1918 he had passed out with the rank of Telegraphist and been assigned as a signals clerk on the SS *Queen*.

The ship had been built at Port Glasgow in 1907 and after a period in British hands, ownership was transferred to The Rome Steam Shipping Company in 1914. On the outbreak of war she was upgraded to a defensively armed merchant ship. On 28th June 1918, while engaged in carrying general cargo and coal from Cardiff to Spezie in Italy,[154] the *Queen* was torpedoed and sunk 130 miles north-west of Cape Vilano in Spain by the German submarine U53.

According to the Admiralty Register of Deaths & Injuries, Frank survived the sinking but was seriously injured. He suffered contusions and lacerations to his left lung and was transferred to the Royal Navy hospital in Gibraltar for treatment. He died from his injuries on 2nd July[155] and was

---

[152] Forces War Records
[153] Ancestry
[154] http://www.naval-history.net/WW1LossesBrMS1918.htm
[155] National Archives Ref ADM 337/43

buried in Gibraltar's North Front Cemetery, where he lies in in Plot C3942. Notification of his death was published in the local Rawtenstall newspaper.[156]

Norman is remembered on the Rawtenstall War Memorial and on the war memorial at Canon Slade School, formerly Bolton Church Institute School. In his research, the late Philip Clark[157] commented that Lionel *"was the only former pupil on the First World War Roll of Honour who had attended Bacup & Rawtenstall Grammar School"* as opposed to Newchurch Grammar School.[158]

North Front Cemetery, Gibraltar [159]

---

[156] Rossendale Free Press: 13th July 1918
[157] P L Clark's research is in the BRGS archives
[158] At that date known as Bacup & Rawtenstall Technical School
[159] Photograph: The War Graves Photographic Project

Chapter 9

One of the repercussions of Germany's return to aggressive submarine warfare was that it gave momentum to Haig's desire for another offensive in Flanders. While the First and Second Battle of Ypres had been German attacks on the allied position in the Salient, the 1917 battle was to be a British attack on German positions.

Flushed with the successes at Messines, Haig planned to attack in Flanders before the autumn weather closed in, with the objective of breaking out from the Ypres salient and outflanking the enemy in the north. Success would ensure the seizure of German submarine bases on the Belgian coast and so neutralise the threat to shipping and supply routes. Since Haig believed the German army was already on the verge of collapse, capturing the ports would lead, ultimately, to an allied victory and the end of the conflict.

Haig has been criticised for not building on the success of Messines by continuing the attack in Flanders immediately. With the ground around Ypres flat and open, the Germans could watch as preparations were being made and so deduce that an attack was imminent. Haig's belief that the German army was on the verge of collapse proved to be unfounded and the seven week lull allowed them to strengthen their defences in preparation for the allied attack.

The Third Battle of Ypres began on 31st July 1917. During the two week preliminary bombardment, 3,000 British guns fired 4.5 million shells on enemy positions. Better known as the Battle of Passchendaele, the campaign has gone down in history not only for the appalling number of casualties on both sides but for the terrible conditions, principally mud, in which men fought.

Although the battle began well for the Allies, bad weather soon ensured that both sides became bogged down. The weather in the first few months of the year had been poor but it now took a turn for the worse. The rain that began on the night of 31 July was the heaviest to fall in Flanders in thirty years and the summer of 1917 as a whole proved to be the wettest there for 75 years. The water table around Ypres is very high and the majority of the drainage systems had been destroyed in the bombardment. As the rain continued, the constant heavy shelling from both sides churned the thick, clay soil into a sticky quagmire leaving a landscape pockmarked with deep, water-filled shell holes. The whole battlefield was turned into a vast sea of mud that sucked wounded men and exhausted animals to their deaths. Wooden duckboards had been laid down as pathways across the mud to ease the passage across the battlefield. Should anyone fall off them, orders had been issued that no rescue was to be attempted, due to the danger that the rescuer might also succumb to the mud. One can only imagine the thoughts of soldiers who had to leave their comrades behind, some pleading to be shot rather than be left to drown in mud.

Digging trenches in which to shelter from the incessant shelling and horrendous weather was nigh impossible and lighting fires as a source of warmth, for cooking or for drying wet, mud-caked uniforms was forbidden. Troops sought what little cover they could find in water-filled shell holes, where they huddled together in a vain attempt to keep warm. The muddy conditions made it almost impossible to manoeuvre artillery into new positions; whole gun carriages could be sucked under the mud. Horses struggled to gain a foothold in the sticky slime, often sinking up to their bellies in the quagmire, with the consequence that food and equipment wagons were delayed or never arrived.

September was certainly drier but the ground took time to dry out and any semblance of roads had long since disappeared. Caked, dried mud clung to kit and equipment, clogged guns and rifles and made life almost impossible for those who were simply trying to survive in the hell of the shattered landscape. Despite mounting losses and very few gains, Haig refused to accept defeat and call off the attack, preferring to launch further assaults in the hope of success.

As the battle entered its third month in October, there was still no appreciable progress towards the planned objectives. With the approach of winter and with casualties continuing to mount, morale among the physically exhausted troops fell. On 13th October, Haig's commanders were at last able to persuade him that, once a suitable position had been reached where they could hold the line, the campaign would be put on hold until the weather improved the following spring. A combined force of British and Canadian troops eventually captured the shattered village of Passchendaele on 6th November and when the remaining piece of relatively high ground was captured on 10th November, the battle was called off.

Passchendaele is remembered today as one of the bloodiest battles of the First World War. It had taken three months and six days to advance a mere five miles and by the time the campaign ended, allied casualties amounted to 250,000 men killed, wounded or missing. German casualties are estimated to have been in the region of 200,000.[160]

In 1918, the Allies were faced with the need to reorganise their defences in the face of the German Spring Offensive and, without a single shot being fired, withdrew from the area of Flanders that had been won at such a high price during 1917.

---

[160] iwm.org.uk

Four of the former pupils fought and died in the Flanders region during the Third Battle of Ypres. Two lie in CWGC cemeteries; one in French and one in Belgian Flanders.[161] The other two were among the many thousands of troops missing in Flanders who have no known grave. They are both remembered on the Tyne Cot Memorial close to Ypres. Today the CWGC commemorates over 76,000 allied troops who died in Flanders during the Third Battle of Ypres. Over half have no known grave and are remembered on Memorials to the Missing.

A British tank marooned in a sea of mud[162]

---

[161] Today Flanders is the autonomous north region of Belgium but in 1917 it was an area that covered northern France and southern Belgium.
[162] By kind permission of The Keasbury-Gordon Photographic Archive

Private John Edward Winterbottom
8th Battalion, East Lancashire Regiment
Died 2nd August 1917

Outersteene Communal Cemetery
Bailleul, France

John Winterbottom was born on 18th March 1898 in Whitewell Bottom, a hamlet near the small Lancashire village of Lumb-in-Rossendale.[163] He was the eldest son of Robert Winterbottom and his wife Mary Ann, who farmed land at Higher Walls, land previously farmed by Robert's father. John began his education at Lumb Church of England School and was admitted to Newchurch Grammar School on 22nd March 1911. Nothing has been found to indicate how long he was at school or what he did when he left.

Despite a rigorous search, few details have been found that relate to either John's civilian or military life. No records have been lodged at the National Archives and a search of local newspapers failed to find a report of his death or an

---

[163] In the valley of the Whitewell Brook, about 4 miles from Rawtenstall

obituary. The little information that was discovered came from the CWGC and the Forces War Records websites. The CWGC database showed that he had served as a Private in the 8th battalion, East Lancashire Regiment and was issued with service number 37177 while the military genealogical website Forces War Records provided the additional detail that he had joined the army at Preston.

Unfortunately there is nothing to say when John joined up but if certain parameters are followed, it is possible to give a rough estimate. Legally, a prospective soldier had to be eighteen, although it is true that some young boys lied about their age in their eagerness to enlist. For the purposes of this exercise it has been assumed that John wasn't a boy soldier and so the earliest he could have joined up would have been his eighteenth birthday. This fell a few months after conscription had been introduced in 1916.

By the terms of the Military Service Act, all men who were legally eligible for conscription as at 1st March 1916 were deemed to have passed into the army reserve. Those under eighteen were allocated to a specific class, dependent on their year of birth, and were called up automatically when they reached eighteen. John's date of birth would have seen him allocated to Class 4 and entered into the reserve on 18th March 1916. He would then have waited to be called up when there was space at a training base to accommodate him.

Since no service record has survived, the battalion's official history and war diaries have been studied in an effort to understand what battalion life might have been like for John. Until September 1916, when the Training Reserve was introduced, new recruits were sent to their battalion's reserve for training. There they would build up their fitness, learn drill and marching skills, field craft and army discipline. A more intensive period followed, concentrating on the handling and maintenance of weapons. Having mastered these basics, a soldier was posted to one of the specialist training centres to learn a specific 'trade' such as artillery, signals, map reading, catering or transport, and only at the end of this period would he be posted to a service battalion. Despite basic and advanced training lasting upwards of six months, new soldiers often arrived at the front unprepared for war. If the training schedule illustrated above is taken as a guide, John could have arrived at his battalion in early 1917.

The 8th East Lancashire Regiment had embarked for the front at the end of July 1915 and fought at the Battles of the Somme and the Ancre. In March 1917, they relocated away from the Somme and took part in the Battle of Arras. During these operations the battalion spent time in both the front and reserve lines and came under enemy fire on many occasions, suffering a large number of casualties. They were later withdrawn behind Arras where they took part in high intensity training exercises. These sessions occupied most of the troops' waking hours. A large number of the men felt the training was excessive and far too strenuous. Relieved when orders were received to move north,[164] their pleasure may have been short-lived when they learned they were bound for the Ypres Salient.

The battalion's arrival in the Salient came as plans were being finalised for the third Ypres offensive. The 8th East Lancs were to take part in a number of diversionary attacks on the enemy's flanks. The first of these took place on the first day of the main attack on 31st July. The original orders were for the whole battalion to push forward, reconnoitre the locality and investigate the strength of the enemy. This was later amended to say that patrols of no more than platoon strength were to be sent out along the whole front.[165] The

---

[164] The History of the East Lancashire Regiment – 8th battalion Littlebury Bros, Liverpool 1936
[165] A platoon was made up of approximately fifty soldiers

battalion's commanding officer reported back to headquarters that this was an impossible task as the strength of the enemy's artillery barrage would result in very heavy casualties. After a period of consultation, the attack was postponed until an allied barrage could be put up to cover the East Lancs' advance.

The men went over the top at 8am on 31st July and although their objectives were met, they suffered heavy casualties, losing all but three of their officers. When the enemy were observed preparing to counter-attack later in the day, the remaining officers had to consider the battalion's position. After a day of incessant rain, hardly a rifle or Lewis gun was capable of firing because their barrels and mechanisms were completely clogged with mud. Unable to establish contact with the units on either flank, and in urgent need of reinforcements, they considered it unlikely they could hold off the enemy and so ordered the battalion to withdraw at 10.45pm. They remained in the front line during the next day before they were relieved on the night of 1st August and returned to their billets behind the lines.

No information has been found to indicate what happened to John Winterbottom but the CWGC database records that he died on 2nd August 1917, the day after his battalion returned to camp. He was only 19 years old, the minimum age at which a soldier could legally be sent overseas to fight, and so may only have been at the front for a short period. The battalion diary noted that search parties were sent out on the morning of 1st August and that they had brought in all the wounded from the day before.[166]

John may have been among the wounded brought in from the battlefield as the Register of Soldiers' Effects states that he died from wounds. He is buried in Plot 1.A.3 at

---

[166] National Archives Ref WO 95/25374

Outtersteene Communal Cemetery Extension at Bailleul. The cemetery was used by Nos 1, 2 and 53 Australian Casualty Clearing Stations from July 1917 and it is possible John was taken to one of these units although Plots 1, 11 and 14 were also used after the war to concentrate the burials brought in from the surrounding battlefield and smaller cemeteries.

John's name was one of those inscribed on the memorial board installed in the porch at St Michael and All Angels Church, Lumb. The porch was built in honour of the forty-nine men from this small Lancashire village who died in the Great War. The church has since been deconsecrated and the memorial is now located at Whittaker Museum in Rawtenstall.

Outtersteene Communal Cemetery Extension

Private Percy Horsfield
21st Battalion, Manchester Regiment
Died 4th October 1917

Remembered
Tyne Cot Memorial

Percy was the only son of John and Mary Horsfield who lived at 8 Pleasant View, Waterfoot. He was born on 20th February 1894. His father was a cotton mule spinner and the family worshipped at Bethlehem Unitarian Church in Newchurch. He attended Waterfoot Council School and was admitted to NGS on 8th May 1906. In 1909, John Horsfield died at the age of 47, leaving his wife to look after their two children. By the 1911 census, Percy and his elder sister were employed at a local slipper mill; Percy as a clicker[167] and his sister as a sewing machinist.

---

[167] One who cuts the uppers from a skin of leather. The name originated in the days before mechanisation when the operator's hand-knife blade rattled against the brass plate used to protect the patterns that were laid on top of the leather.

Percy's service records are very badly scorched but they show that he joined up at Rawtenstall on 11th December 1915. He was accepted into the East Lancashire Regiment as Private 25019 on 16th March 1916. He joined under the 'Derby Scheme', a scheme in operation between 16th October and 15th December 1915. Introduced by Lord Derby in an effort to increase recruitment, men had the choice of continuing to enlist voluntarily or to attest with the obligation of being called up at a later date. To ensure training bases were not flooded with new recruits, those who deferred were put into call-up groups dependent on their date of birth. On completion of his training, he embarked for France on 4th July and was attached to the 17th Manchester battalion with service number 43164. He was officially transferred to the battalion on 1st September.

Medical records indicate that Percy was treated at a couple of Field Ambulances during October and November before he was admitted to 39 CCS on 28th October with suspected dysentery. He was transferred to No 9 General Hospital at Rouen, where the diagnosis was confirmed. Evacuated on the hospital ship *Gloucester Castle* on 21st November, he was admitted to University General Hospital, and remained there until he was discharged on 12 January 1917.

He returned to duty on 7th February and remained in England until he embarked for Boulogne on 2nd May. On arrival in France, he travelled to No 30 Infantry Base Depot at Etaples, one of a number of holding camps near the channel where soldiers were kept in training until they received a new posting. Percy was posted to 21st Manchester battalion and joined them in the field on 26th May.

The 21st battalion (also known as the 6th City Battalion) had seen action on the Somme, where they captured the village of Mametz and took part in the fighting at Bazentin, High Wood, Delville Wood and Guillemont. They remained in the area, where they witnessed the German withdrawal to the Hindenburg Line and took part in the Battle of Arras. Percy joined them around this time, just before they were sent into Belgium to join an allied force preparing for the renewed attack in the area around Ypres.

There is very little detail in the battalion war diary for the day Percy died, simply a short entry noting that the battalion was 'in action'; however, the entries for the days prior to the attack give a fuller account. On 1st October 1917, the battalion was holding the line east of Polygon Wood, near the town of Zonnebeke. Their orders were to attack the slightly higher ground to the south of Polygon Wood, move north past Zonnebeke and then on towards the village of Poelcappelle[168]. The aim was to forestall any planned German attack and force them to retreat from their positions on the higher ground overlooking Ypres. As a precursor to the British attack, a huge artillery bombardment would open up and then, as the British troops moved forward, their positions would be screened from the enemy by a creeping barrage.

On 1st October, the 21st Manchester regiment began to move forward under cover of darkness and, by the night of 2nd, men from both the 21st and 22nd battalions were sheltering as best they could in filthy dugouts at Zillebeke Lake. They started to move eastwards towards their assembly points within Polygon Wood late in the evening of 3rd October and were in position by 2.30am the next morning.

The battle plan for 4th October called for the 22nd battalion to go over in the first wave. Percy and his comrades in the 21st battalion were to wait until they were called on for "mopping up purposes" as the attack progressed. The main attack was launched at 6am and the 22nd battalion soon came under very heavy artillery fire and enfilade machine gun fire.

---

[168] This attack on 4th October 1917 is known to historians as the Battle of Broodseinde.

With losses mounting, a company of the 21st battalion was sent forward in support at 9.30am, followed by a further company early in the afternoon. The conditions in which the troops now found themselves were terrible. It had been raining since early morning and they had very little shelter from the cold and rain in the sea of mud that was the Flanders battlefield.

This attack, the Battle of Broodseinde, was a great allied success. Despite the desperate conditions the troops experienced, it proved to be the most successful assault during the Third Battle of Ypres and was due to the implementation of "bite and hold" tactics. These ensured that objectives were limited to those that could be successfully defended against a German counter-attack.

Twenty-three year old Percy Horsfield was killed during the Battle of Broodseinde. Although the CWGC records list him as a casualty of 4th October, the UK Army Register of Soldiers' Effects notes that his death occurred "at some time between 4th and 7th October". This clearly illustrates the confusion that often existed during and after a battle and how difficult it was to pinpoint the exact date of death. This was generally the case when the death hadn't been witnessed or where a soldier was initially reported missing.

Notification of Percy's death was published in the Bacup Times and this included the information that, after she received notification of her son's death, Mrs Horsfield had received a letter from an officer in his company. He had expressed his condolences and explained that Percy's trench had received a direct hit during a period of heavy enemy shelling. The officer advised the family that, regretfully, Percy's body hadn't been recovered.[169] Additional details were found in the BRGS archives.[170] Percy had been in a group of

---

[169] Bacup Times: 20th October 1917
[170] Friends of BRGS newsletter No 16, Winter 2008 page 7

soldiers who had been sent out to a listening post forward of the line. While they were entrenched there, the post had been shelled and all the occupants had been buried by the subsequent falling debris.

The war diary details the casualties for the 4th October as: one officer and 35 OR[171] killed; 6 officers and 148 OR wounded and 19 missing. Percy's body was never found. He is one of some 35,000 men who fought in Flanders between August 1917 and November 1918 and who have no known grave. They are remembered on the Tyne Cot Memorial which forms the eastern boundary wall in Tyne Cot Cemetery near Ypres.

In 1921, Bethlehem Unitarian Church dedicated a stained glass window as a memorial to Percy and the other church members who had died in the conflict. The church was demolished in 1987 and it is thought that the memorial was lost at that time.[172]

HORSFIELD P.

Tyne Cot Memorial Inscription

---

[171] other ranks
[172] http://www.rossendalefhhs.org.uk/files/war_memorials

Gunner Albert Wray Titterington
177th Siege Battery, Royal Garrison Artillery
Died 5th October 1917

Reservoir Cemetery
Ypres, Belgium

Albert Wray Titterington[173] was born in Carlisle, his mother's hometown, on 9th September 1891. He began his schooling at Waterfoot Council School and he was admitted to Newchurch Grammar School on 16th January 1904. Before the Great War intervened, he worked as a tailor in his father's outfitters shop in Waterfoot. He attended St James' Church, where he sang in the choir, and was a popular member of Waterfoot Liberal Club.

Albert's service record still survives although it contains little more than basic information. He enlisted at Bacup on 28th February 1916, after conscription was introduced, and was immediately posted to the reserves. He was called up in June and travelled to No 2 Depot, Royal Garrison Artillery (RGA) at Fort Brockhurst, Gosport and began his basic training there on 22nd June. A period of gunnery training

---

[173] Photograph: Rossendale Free Press

followed and having completed this successfully, he was posted to the 177th Siege Battery, RGA on 20th August.

As Gunner 103094, Albert left England on 25th September 1916 and landed in France the following day. There is little in his service record that relates directly to his overseas service, but the 177th Siege Battery's war diary gives a clear illustration of what daily life was like.[174]

Entries begin on 10th October, at which date the 177th battery was in billets at Bienvillers, about 20km south west of Arras. Heavy shelling throughout the night had left one gunner dead and eleven others wounded and as a result, the billets were evacuated. The following day, a party was ordered back to recover the unit's rations. Just how hazardous the situation was is evidenced by the fact that five of the men were killed on the return journey.

Siege Batteries such as the one Albert joined were part of the army's heavy artillery and were positioned some way behind the lines. They were equipped with howitzers[175] which fired large-calibre, high-explosive shells. These had enormous destructive capability and were an efficient means of disrupting or destroying enemy artillery, supply routes and communications.[176] Moving howitzers to a new location was neither a quick nor an easy process. It involved each of the guns being attached to a limber[177] and pulled to the new location by a team of horses, often over rough or waterlogged ground. Once at a new location, the gunners would spend many hours registering their guns[178] before they could

---

[174] National Archives Ref WO95/296/3
[175] Howitzers fired their projectiles over relatively high trajectories with a steep angle of descent.
[176] The Long Long Trail - longlongtrail.co.uk: The Role of the Siege Battery
[177] A two-wheeled cart used to support the gun when it is relocated
[178] The gunners fired ranging shots at a target which could be observed and adjustments were then made to aid accuracy.

be fired in earnest. Although located away from the front line, the heavy brigades were still in dangerous territory, regularly coming under sustained, heavy shelling from the enemy's artillery as they attempted to destroy the allied gun positions.

Artillery unit war diaries often included daily reports on how often and for how long the guns had opened up on any particular day and the number of shells that had been fired in that time. A reading of the diary for the 177th battery during the late autumn of 1916, shows that firing reached a peak at 5.45am on 13 November when a very heavy bombardment was put up during the closing stages of the first Battle of the Somme. That morning, 614 rounds were fired; a considerable effort for all involved. At other times of the year it seemed to fluctuate between quiet periods, with little or no firing, and periods of heavy activity. Early 1917 seems to have been quieter and the men spent their time improving their surroundings and building dugouts in which to shelter not only from enemy shells but also from the atrocious winter weather.

Albert's Active Service Casualty Form is in his file and shows that he was admitted to hospital on 11th March 1917 when suffering from PUO - pyrexia (fever) of unknown origin. He was released back to his unit on 19th March, just as his battery moved to an advance position nearer Arras. On arrival, they received official orders that, due to impending action, it was imperative that all guns had sufficient ammunition available. The battery officer ordered that nothing was to divert the men from this task, and at least two daily trips to the ammunition dumps were to be made under cover of darkness. If this proved impossible, then the trips were to be carried out in daylight. This was a far more dangerous operation, as there was a greater likelihood that they would be spotted and fired upon.

On 4th April, the battery received notice of an imminent allied attack and commenced a heavy and focussed artillery barrage on the enemy's positions. When the Battle of Arras began on 9th April, the batteries fired thousands of rounds in support of the infantry. This intensity continued into May as the guns targeted enemy artillery and troop positions. On 11th May, the battery suffered numerous casualties as a result of heavy enemy shelling and this shellfire increased in momentum in the following weeks.

The Third Battle of Ypres had begun on 31st July and towards the end of August, Albert's unit was moved from Arras to new firing locations near Poperinghe, about 7 miles west of Ypres. As the battle continued, artillery on both sides fired more and more frequently and for far longer periods. The enemy increasingly targeted allied artillery positions and many gunners were killed by direct hits on their gun positions.

A specific incident, relating directly to Albert, is related in the unit's war diary. At about 2pm on 5th October, a casualty report came in. Earlier that day, a party had been sent out to take ammunition up to the guns in one of the forward positions. They were hit by enemy fire, which resulted in the deaths of a bombardier and two gunners and the wounding of a Lieutenant and four gunners. The diary named Gunner Titterington as one of the injured.[179]

There is confusion as to what happened to Albert after this. A local Rossendale newspaper[180] carried a report that the first his parents heard about their son's injury was in letters sent home by two local soldiers. Gunner Shenton, from Crawshawbooth, confirmed Albert had been wounded and that he had seen him picked up and taken to hospital. The report makes no mention of the hospital's location. A second

---

[179] National Archives Ref WO95/296/3
[180] Rossendale Free Press: 27th October 1917

soldier, Private Ashford of Cloughfold, wrote that he knew Albert had been seriously wounded.[181] Despite making great efforts, three weeks later Albert's parents were still waiting to hear what had happened to their son. All that they knew was that he had been posted as 'missing' in the War Office Daily list published on 9th November 1917[182].

A second newspaper report some weeks later[183] told of another local soldier who had read that Albert was missing. Sometime later, while he was at Ypres, he had noticed a grave cross bearing the name AW *Tatterton*. Recognising the similarity of the name, he noted down the service number, battery and regiment that were inscribed on the cross and when he was next home on leave, he visited Albert's parents and gave them this information. Other than the surname, the details on the cross were exactly the same as Albert's. Armed with this information, his parents made further enquiries and eventually received the official news that their son had died on 6th October from wounds he had received the previous day.

Albert's service file at Kew includes a casualty report. Written by a burial officer in the II Anzac Corps[184] and dated 8th October, the date of death is given as "on or shortly after 6th October", although the date engraved on Albert's headstone and noted in the CWGC database is 5th October, the day he was wounded. This discrepancy is understandable, considering the huge number of casualties that were being brought into the medical units during the battle. The official recorded total for British and Empire troops killed, wounded or missing during the Third Battle of Ypres was reported to be 244,897. Priority had to be given to treating and caring for

---

[181] Rossendale Free Press: 27th October 1917
[182] War Office Daily List 5142 - Forces War Records website
[183] Rossendale Free Press: 8th December 1917
[184] Four NZ Field Ambulance units were located around Ypres in 1917.

the wounded. Records were often completed later, sometimes days later, resulting in this type of error.

Albert was 26 when he died. He is buried in plot 1.E.80 at Ypres Reservoir Cemetery. He was an only child and a *"quiet and much esteemed young man."*[185] When news broke that he was missing, his parents received many messages of hope that he would be found quickly, and on learning of his death, the Rossendale Free Press commented that he was *"an especially well known young man in Waterfoot and being of a quiet and courteous disposition, was much esteemed and respected."*[186] Shortly afterwards, Waterfoot Liberal Club flew a flag at half-mast in memory of their well-respected former member.

Albert's Grave in Ypres Reservoir Cemetery

---

[185] Rossendale Free Press: 27th October 1917
[186] Ibid 8th December 1917

Lance Corporal Arthur Taylor
2/4th Battalion, East Lancashire Regiment
Died 9th October 1917

Remembered
Tyne Cot Memorial

Born on 31st March 1897, Arthur Taylor grew up at 5 Back Church Street in Newchurch, Rossendale and was the elder son of James William and his wife Alice. First educated at junior school in Newchurch, he was admitted to Newchurch Grammar School as a 'Rushton Scholar' in 1908.[187] He was a member at St Nicholas Church, Newchurch and sang in the choir. Although the 1911 census gave his occupation as an office boy, by the time he joined the Army he was working in the lasting room at Hardman's, a local shoe firm in Waterfoot. Shortly before his death, he had sent a letter to Mr Hardman and his former colleagues and had wished them *".... the best of luck, health and prosperity,"* concluding with *"Au Revoir"*.[188]

According to newspaper reports, the news of Arthur's death first reached his family in a letter from a Private

---

[187] No information has been found that relates to this scholarship
[188] Rossendale Free Press: 3rd November 1917

Cockerill, formerly of St James Street in Waterfoot and was confirmed officially a few days later. Aged 20 when he was killed, Arthur had been in the army since early summer 1916 and served with the 2/4th East Lancashire Regiment. He went out to France in March 1917 and had been promoted to Lance Corporal shortly before his death.[189] Of the forty-three names on the school WW1 roll of honour, Arthur Taylor's history was one of the most difficult to research. The circumstances of his death are unknown and his body, if ever found, remained unidentified.

There are 638 soldiers with the name 'A Taylor' on the CWGC database, three of whom served in the East Lancashire Regiment during the First World War. Of these, one had died at Gallipoli in 1915 and could be discounted immediately while another had been born in Burnley to parents whose forenames didn't match those of the Arthur Taylor from Newchurch. The final candidate was a Lance Corporal who had the service number, 202186. He had served with the 2/4th East Lancs and had died on 9th October 1917. This certainly appeared to be a match for Arthur, but the Register of Soldiers' Effects[190] was scrutinised as a final check. Searching using the third soldier's service number, this deceased soldier's next of kin was stated to be his father, one James W Taylor. The correct man had been identified.

The 2/4th East Lancs formed in Blackburn in September 1914. As a second line unit and part of the territorial force, the battalion's job was to undertake home defence and allow regular, first line troops to be released for overseas service. By March 1916 it had become apparent that many second line troops would also be required to serve abroad, and in preparation for this, the 2/4th battalion moved to

---

[189] Rossendale Free Press: 3rd November 1917
[190] Ancestry/UK website

Colchester[191] where the troops spent the next year under training, in readiness for their departure for the Western Front. Embarkation orders were received in late February and the battalion landed at Le Havre on 2nd March 1917.

Although his service record has not survived, the battalion history and war diary explain what Arthur would have experienced while with his unit. The first few weeks were spent near Bethune in northern France, where the troops found much work had to be done bringing the trenches they were to occupy back up to a reasonable standard.

In July, they had moved to within a mile of the Belgian border and were busy constructing a light railway. They later came under the orders of the Royal Engineers, assisting with road construction and building a pontoon across a nearby river. This preparatory work was to ensure that supply lines remained available to support the forthcoming attacks in Flanders. By September, the battalion was back in the front line, in trenches on the Belgian border.

The weather, which had been a little better in September, now took a turn for the worse, and torrential rain returned on 5th October. An attack on the village of Poelcappelle[192] was planned for the 9th of the month and on the 6th the 2/4th East Lancs moved into the area, under orders to bivouac in a field near the Menin Gate. With no shelter other than groundsheets, the battalion waited for two days in the mud and rain before they moved forward towards their attack positions. When they reached the Frezenberg Ridge, they waited for the guide who would take them to their final jumping-off positions under cover of darkness. While they waited, the battalion suffered 20 casualties due to persistent enemy shelling.

---

[191] Some 20,000 troops were garrisoned in the town during the Great War.
[192] The modern day spelling is Poelkapelle

At 6pm on 8th October, the battalion began to traverse the sea of mud in single file. Although they only had to travel about a mile, due to the darkness and the terrible conditions underfoot, the journey took 11 hours. Zero hour was planned for 5.20am, giving the men no time to rest after the journey. Two other battalions were due to attack alongside the East Lancs. When they did not arrive at their positions in time, the 2/4th East Lancs were ordered to spread themselves out more thinly along the line in an effort to cover the gaps.

The official history of the East Lancashire Regiment praised the men who went into the attack at Poelcappelle for their great fortitude and courage.[193] They went into the attack without the expected support on their flank and were cold, wet and almost exhausted, having been given nothing to sustain them after their long march, other than tea.[194] Despite this, they succeeded in reaching and then consolidating their first objective, but were unable to move forward from there due to severe machine gun fire and sniper action. At dusk, they successfully repulsed a strong German counter-attack, and although many of the troops had become separated and were coming under persistent heavy fire, they still managed to hold the line throughout that night and all of the next day.

The only way to get water to the front was by mule train, and although many of these were sent out, few reached their destination. The battalion was relieved on the night of 10th October, but came under heavy shellfire on their way back to the reserve trenches.

2/4th East Lancashire casualties at the battle of Poelcappelle amounted to 13 officers and 316 other ranks killed, wounded or missing. At the end of the engagement,

---

[193] History of the East Lancashire Regiment, Volume II Chapter III
[194] The muddy conditions had made it impossible for supplies to reach troops on time or at the correct point along the line, as supply wagons and horses were constantly bogged down in the mud.

Arthur Taylor was one of those listed as missing although there are no records to say when this might have occurred. He has no known grave, but is remembered on the East Lancs section of the Memorial to the Missing within Tyne Cot cemetery. He is one of almost 35,000 missing officers and men remembered at Tyne Cot who died in the Flanders area after 16th August 1917 and who have no known grave[195]

On the centenary of the battle of Passchendaele in October 2017, the Lancashire Post published a series of articles about Lancashire regiments and the part they played in the Third Battle of Ypres. One discussed the part the 2/4th East Lancs battalion had played in the Battle of Poelcappelle.[196] Within the article is a quote from Philip Gibbs, a war correspondent at the time. Reporting in 'The Times' shortly after the attack he wrote of the "*heroic*" night march the 2/4th East Lancs had made to get to the front and declared *"Nothing better than this has been done and Lancashire should thrill to the tale of it because her sons were its heroes."*[197]

Tyne Cot Memorial Inscription

---

[195] Those who died in Flanders before this date are remembered on the Menin Gate in the centre of Ypres.
[196] www.lep.co.uk/heritage-and-retro/retro/superhuman-bravery-lancashires-men-653826
[197] Ibid

Chapter 10

Although an enormous number of men were killed on the battlefields, thousands more were wounded so badly that they died at aid posts or field ambulances at the front or on their way along the medical evacuation chain. Many survived long enough to reach one of the Casualty Clearing Stations (CCS), only to succumb to their injuries despite the best efforts of the medical staff. Troops also died from illness or disease, in accidents of varying kinds or as a result of gas attacks.

There was also a small group of thirty-seven men who were executed by the British for the capital crimes of murder and mutiny, crimes for which they would also have received the death penalty in peacetime. Disturbingly, however, in addition to these convicted felons, another 306 men were shot for breaches of military discipline - crimes such as desertion, cowardice, falling asleep at their post and insubordination. Allowed legal representation but no right of appeal, they were condemned to death by courts martial. The death sentence was confirmed by Sir Douglas Haig, often in the evening of the same day, and they were executed at dawn the following morning by a firing squad selected from members of their own unit.

When a man was executed, his relatives were advised only that he had died. They were neither informed of the court martial proceedings nor the reasons for it. Often the first a family knew of the circumstances of their loved one's death was when they applied for, and were refused, a war pension. On discovering the truth, most kept it hidden from a sense of shame, and many did so until the day they died. On finding out a relative's fate, a family could request that the reason was added to the inscription on the man's headstone, but in reality only one family did so and the CWGC agreed to their request.[198]

Although the crimes were legally punishable by death at the time they were committed, it is now recognised that some of the men were suffering from shell shock, the equivalent of today's combat stress, and should not have been held responsible for their actions.

When official war memorials were erected around the country after the war, the names of those who had been executed were intentionally omitted. This failing has now been addressed by a new memorial which was unveiled at the National Arboretum in Staffordshire in 2001. It incorporates the statue of a blindfolded soldier in front of 306 wooden posts, each carrying the name of one of the executed men.

In 2007, after a long public campaign on behalf of those 'Shot at Dawn', the government agreed to grant a pardon to all the men, with the exception of those who had been found guilty of murder.

National Arboretum Shot at Dawn Memorial[199]

---

[198] Pte Albert Ingham, 10495 Bailleulmont Communal Cemetery
[199] Picture by kind permission of Anne & David (Use Albums) @ Creative Commons.org - Licence CC PDM 1.0

2ⁿᵈ Lieutenant Jesse Hargreaves Temperley
92ⁿᵈ Company, Machine Gun Corps
Died 25ᵗʰ October 1917

Roclincourt Military Cemetery
Pas de Calais, France

Jessie Temperley[200] was born on 9ᵗʰ January 1889 into a well-known Bacup family, owners of the Cloughhead Mine at Sharneyford. His parents, John & Sarah, had farmed about 13 acres of land at Heap Hey before John joined his elder brother William in running Thomas Temperley & Sons. By 1911, John Temperley was manager at the sanitary pipe manufacturing arm of the business based at the Cloughhead mine. The couple had six children, of whom Jesse was the youngest.

Jesse began his junior education at Sharneyford Board School and won a half share in a scholarship to Newchurch Grammar School. After he left, he took up a clerical job in the town clerk's office at Bacup, later moving to a more senior position as Chief Assistant to the town clerk at

---

[200] Photograph: Bacup Times 10 November 1917

Rochdale Council in 1910. After his death, he was said to have been held in high regard there. He had made plenty of friends among his colleagues and was remembered as having a pleasant disposition.[201]

Responding early to Lord Kitchener's call, Jesse enlisted at Manchester on 5th September 1914. Records at the National Archives indicate that he joined the 20th Royal Fusiliers (Public Schools' Battalion) and was issued with the service number 5795.[202] Part of the 33rd Division, the battalion trained at Clipstone, near Mansfield, before they moved down to Salisbury Plain in August 1915. Here they carried out final training and firing practice before they embarked for France on 14th November.

After his death, a local newspaper reported that Jesse had seen 'considerable service' in France and had been wounded on the Somme.[203] His papers at the National Archives provided additional information. On 20th July 1916, during the attack on High Wood, Jesse was wounded in the buttocks and right foot. He entered the evacuation chain, eventually reaching one of the Base Hospitals at Rouen. His injuries were sufficiently serious for him to be evacuated back to England on the hospital ship *St Andrew*, which left France on 25th July.[204] On his arrival in England he was assessed as category D (unfit for service but likely to recover within six months) and following a period of recuperation, was posted to the 6th (Reserve) battalion, Royal Fusiliers on 26th October 1916. His Medal Index card indicates he was given the new service number GS/47443 on joining the Fusiliers.

Recommended for a commission by his superiors, his application is in his file at Kew. Dated 11th October 1916,

---

[201] Haslingden Guardian: 9th November 1917
[202] National Archives Ref WO 339/81690
[203] Haslingden Guardian: 9th November 1917
[204] National Archives WO 339/81690

Jesse stated that his order of preference was to serve with the Artillery or the Machine Gun Corps. He was accepted into the latter and ordered to report for officer training at the Machine Gun depot at Bisley on 1st January 1917. Commissioned on 26th April, he spent a few days at home in Lancashire before going to Mansfield for additional training.[205]

2nd Lieutenant Temperley left England on 1st July 1917 and travelled to Camiers, the Machine Gun Corps' base depot just north of Étaples. On 11th July he was sent to 92 Company, Machine Gun Corps, who were in billets to the west of Arras. The Company war diary shows that three days later the unit moved into the front line, and Jesse took command of No 1 section.[206]

Over the next few months, the diary records the Corps' movements. They moved in and out of the front line on a regular cycle and on 14th July, came under enemy fire from both the German trenches and enemy aircraft. These attacks resulted in many casualties. When the men were in their billets, a more normal pattern of army life continued, with time spent cleaning kit and gun limbers, church and inspection parades, training courses, gun practices and sports events. There was even the opportunity for some of the men to go on all too infrequent leave.

Life in the trenches could be difficult, unpleasant and dangerous. To give troops some shelter from enemy fire and the worst of the elements, dugouts were often built into the trench sides or underground. It was common practice to put up gas curtains at the entrances to try to protect those inside from the effects of enemy gas attacks. On 24th October 1917, Jesse's unit were in the front line near Arras, and after coming off duty, Jesse and two Privates, one his batman,

---

[205] Bacup Times: 10th November 1917
[206] National Archives WO95/2358/2

retired to their dugout to rest. What followed was explained to Jesse's parents in a letter written by his Commanding Officer, Captain Nicholas A Johns.[207] Since it was a cold night, the men asked for a brazier of burning coals to be brought in. Sometime between midnight and one o'clock, one of the soldiers woke up and *"found himself exhausted due to an accumulation of gas from the fire."*[208] He struggled out of the dugout and into the fresh air and once slightly recovered, went back in to assist Jesse and his batman. Both were unconscious and, being too weak to get them out by himself, the soldier went for help. A short time later, the two men were dragged out of the dugout, and although his batman was still breathing, Jesse was found to be unresponsive. A doctor was called to the scene but Jesse could not be resuscitated.

The Corps' war diary refers to a Court of Enquiry having been held and the result forwarded to headquarters through "the usual channels."[209] The full report from the enquiry is at the National Archives and includes hand-written statements taken from all those involved in the rescue, including the Medical Officer, Captain Alexander of the 18th West Yorkshire Regiment. It was he who had attempted resuscitation.[210]

Arriving at 2am, Captain Alexander had gone down into the dugout and on examining Jesse had found no signs of life. In his medical opinion, the cause of death was carbon monoxide poisoning. The court concluded that because the fire was in the alcove beside Jesse, and his sleeping area was screened off from the rest of the room by the gas curtains, carbon monoxide had built up to a greater extent there than in the outer area where the two privates were sleeping. This

---

[207] Haslingden Guardian: 9th November 1917
[208] Ibid
[209] National Archives WO95/2358/2
[210] National Archives Ref WO 339/81690

meant that they were poisoned to a lesser extent, allowing them to recover once they were in the fresh air.

The Enquiry made reference to two earlier but non-fatal incidents where coals had been brought into dugouts. As a consequence of these, an order had been issued to say that no fires were to be burned in dugouts with a single entrance. The court noted that Lt Temperley had initialled an acceptance of this order on 25th July 1917.

Whilst it might appear that Jesse had ignored the order, it had only prohibited fires in dugouts with a *single* entrance and a plan contained within the report papers clearly shows that Jesse's dugout had two entrances.[211] Witnesses confirmed that both of these, and the entrance to Jesse's sleeping area, were covered by gas curtains. This meant that carbon monoxide had built up due to the lack of ventilation.

From a reading of the unit war diary, it can be seen that Captain Johns had only taken command of the company on 20th September.[212] Even in that short time he had come to appreciate Jesse's worth and in writing to Jesse's parents said, *"...what a good fellow he was, and both as an officer in the company and as a friend I shall miss him very much"* [213] The Captain continued, *"We all feel the loss of your son very much and I know he will be very much missed by the men of his section, for he was always persistent in looking after their welfare and his experience in the ranks had undoubtedly taught him how to look after their interests best."*[214] The chaplain also wrote a letter of sympathy in which he referred to Jesse as *"a splendid soldier who was conscientious and dutiful"* and *"well liked by everybody".*[215]

---

[211] There is nothing in the report to indicate whether the order banning fires was later amended to include dugouts with more than one entrance.
[212] National Archives WO 95/2358/2
[213] Haslingden Guardian: 9th November 1917
[214] Ibid
[215] Haslingden Guardian: 9th November 1917

Jesse Temperley was 28 years old when he died. He was buried the day after the accident in an area that now lies within Roclincourt Military Cemetery. The grave is located at plot II.E.2. He is remembered on the Bacup town war memorial and his name is inscribed on the memorial at Christ Church in Bacup.

Roclincourt Military Cemetery

2nd Lieutenant Vernon Radcliffe Stewart
Royal Flying Corps
Died 5th December 1917

Haslingden Cemetery
Rossendale, Lancashire

Vernon Radcliffe Stewart was the son of a Scottish-born physician and surgeon, Dr Barclay Stewart, and his wife Stella. Born in Derby on 19th March 1894, he was the second of five children. Privately educated in his early years, he attended Haslingden Secondary before he moved to Newchurch Grammar School on 6th May 1903. He continued his senior education at Giggleswick School, an independent boarding school in Settle where he excelled at sports.[216] He played cricket for the school's 1st XI and captained the 1st XV rugby team. An accomplished athlete and hockey player, he also played fives and racquet sports and joined the local Kelsal Rugby Club. In addition, he was Colour Sergeant in the school's Officer Training Corps. When Vernon left Giggleswick School, he studied science at Manchester

---
[216] Photograph: Haslingden Guardian

University for two years. This was a foundation for him to study medicine at St Mary's hospital in Paddington, from where he graduated with a Bachelor of Medicine degree in 1912.

On the outbreak of war, Vernon obtained a temporary commission. Gazetted on 12th October 1914, he joined the Army Service Corps (ASC) as a 2nd Lieutenant. The ASC was organised into various companies, each with a specific purpose. Some came under the orders of a Division, while others were under the direct control of Corps, Army or General Headquarters.[217] Vernon's company was part of the 29th Division that sailed to Alexandria on 23 March 1915.

After serving in Egypt, he sailed for Gallipoli on the transport ship HMT *Southland*. On 2nd September 1915, while navigating the waters of Mudros Bay near the Greek island of Lemnos, the ship was struck by a torpedo. Almost immediately she began to list both to starboard and towards the bow. Despite the damage, most of the troops on board were evacuated by lifeboats, while the remainder jumped overboard and clung to wreckage until they were picked up by a hospital ship about two hours later.

An article in the local paper at the time of Vernon's death reported that he had played a prominent part in saving lives during this incident. He had helped launch the lifeboats and then scrambled back to the vessel for his camera in order to take evidential photographs for the Admiralty. Aware that the ship was carrying a considerable amount of money, pay for the many troops fighting in the Dardanelles, he broke down a door, ensuring that over a ton of coin was recovered before the ship foundered. On 15th September he was mentioned in the commanding officer's 'Orders of the Day' for his work during the evacuation, but in a letter home from Gallipoli he

---

[217] The Long Long Trail-longlongtrail.co.uk/army/regiments-and-corps

played down his part, telling his parents he was only doing his duty.[218] In recognition of his work in the Eastern Mediterranean, he was gazetted to the regular army with five year's seniority. [219]

Vernon contracted dysentery and jaundice while at Suvla and was admitted to 26 CCS before he was evacuated from the peninsula. Initially admitted to hospital in Malta, he was invalided home on 28 November and into the care of his father. It was he who wrote to the medical board in January 1916 confirming that his son was free from the infection and, although weak, could be considered fit to return to duty.

Some months later, Vernon transferred to the Royal Flying Corps (RFC) and qualified as a pilot on 5th September. He went to France for advanced training and joined No 9 Wing, 19th Squadron who were based at Savy, south west of Saint-Quentin. Archive records confirm that Vernon's RFC service abroad was cut short. On 2nd October 1916, only a month after he arrived in France, he was admitted to Wimereux General Hospital suffering from severe enteritis and was evacuated back to hospital in Bristol.[220] His file at the National Archives shows that his recovery was slow but, following a period of recuperation at a Southport officers 'convalescent home, he returned to light duties in May 1917. Periods of illness continued to plague him, and after a Medical Board confirmed that he was no longer fit for General Service abroad, he was posted as a flying instructor to No 28 Training Squadron at Castle Bromwich aerodrome.[221]

On 12th July 1917, Vernon was hospitalised with a fracture to the base of his skull following a motor cycle

---

[218] Haslingden Guardian: December 7 1917
[219] National Archives Ref WO 339-10617
[220] Medical record accessed online at Forces War Records
[221] National Archives Ref WO 339-10617

accident on the way home from the aerodrome to his billet.[222] He returned to light duties but was not permitted to fly until he had been assessed by a medical board. This was set for 28th December, but before the board could meet Vernon was accidently killed at the Castle Bromwich aerodrome on 5th December when he was hit by the propeller of a Nieuport aeroplane. He was 23 years old.

Within the many papers in Vernon's file at the National Archives is a rather poignant letter dated 11th January 1918. It is hand-written in French and addressed to the War Office.[223] A lady who lived in Zurich asked for news of Vernon as her own enquiries had come to nothing. It would appear that she had known him for some time as she had two addresses for him: the 29th Division BEF and the Royal Flying School in Upavon, Wiltshire. She asked if someone would be kind enough to take a moment to reply and said she was hoping for good news. The War Office reply was short and to the point. *"The Military Secretary presents his compliments . . . . . and much regrets that 2nd Lt VR Stewart of the Army Service Corps, attached Royal Flying Corps, was struck by the propeller of an aeroplane and killed on the 5th December 1917 at Castle Bromwich, Birmingham."*[224] Undoubtedly this sad news must have come as a shock to her.

Vernon's body was returned home to Haslingden and is buried in the local cemetery. Where a service death occurred in the UK during the First World War, the deceased's family could choose to have a private family burial. In these cases the grave was not marked with a CWGC headstone and the responsibility for maintenance of the plot lay with the family, and not the Commission. Vernon's family chose to bury him

---

[222] A medical board found that no blame for the accident should be apportioned to Vernon
[223] National Archives Ref WO 339-10617
[224] Ibid

privately. His headstone is inscribed with his name and that of two of his siblings, both of whom died from diphtheria on the same day in 1903. In due course, Dr and Mrs Stewart's names were added.

Vernon Stewart is remembered on memorials at Giggleswick School, Manchester University, St Mary's Hospital in Paddington and the Haslingden Roll of Honour.

Stewart Family Headstone
Haslingden Cemetery

Sapper James Arthur Ray
431st Field Company, Royal Engineers
Died 27th December 1917

Lijssenthoek Military Cemetery
Poperinghe, Belgium

James Arthur Ray was born on 11th May 1895. He was the son of Daniel, a Stacksteads joiner and cabinet maker, and his wife Elizabeth. The family initially lived at Plantation Street, Bacup and later moved to 254 Salem Terrace in Stacksteads. The 1911 census records show that the couple had six surviving children - three boys and three girls; James was the third youngest in the family. The NGS admission records hold no information about his education other than that he was admitted to the school on 21st September 1908. When he left, he started work as a warehouse boy in a local cotton factory, later joining his elder brother in their father's carpentry business.

In theory, soldiers who enlisted in the British Army in the early years of the war had a choice as to which regiment they joined, but after conscription was introduced, this was no longer the case. As the war progressed and casualty rates rose, new recruits were assigned as need demanded, although some notice might be taken of any particularly useful skillset a recruit brought from civilian life. James enlisted at Manchester in February 1916 and was posted to the 2/2nd East Lancs Field Company of the Royal Engineers (RE), possibly due to his carpentry skills. After basic training at Manchester, he was posted to the RE divisional base at Cavalry Barracks, Colchester for his advanced training.

Field companies were each assigned to a specific army division, and while at Colchester the 2/2nd East Lancs was attached to the Colchester-based 66th (2nd East Lancashire) Division. A field company supplied their division with a variety of technical skills such as plumbing, electrical, mining, joinery and road building and they worked both behind and in front of the line.

Although James's service record has not survived, his Medal Index Card shows that he was first issued with the service number (T) 3408, the T indicating that he had been assigned to a territorial battalion. In the pre-war army, a territorial soldier was given a new number every time he transferred to a different unit, even if he was moving between battalions of the same regiment. As the war progressed and the number of recruits increased exponentially, the numbering system became so complicated and confusing that administrative errors were commonplace. To simplify matters, a new system was introduced in 1917. Blocks of six-figure service numbers were allocated to all TF units and these remained unchanged when a man was transferred, unless he was transferred out to a different Army Corps. Under this new system, Sapper James Ray's serial number was changed to 440610.

In late February 1917, the 66th Division received orders to embark for France, and by 16th March all men and equipment had landed safely at Le Havre. Shortly before they left Southampton, the 2/2nd East Lancs Field Company was renamed and became the 431st Field Company. On arrival in France, they moved in stages down to the area around Bethune and took up their position at Le Preol, a small hamlet on the outskirts of the town.[225]

Over the following months, the 431st Field Company were kept extremely busy. They dug communication trenches, prepared gun emplacements and constructed a narrow gauge railway. As the front line moved, they built new Divisional headquarters, dugouts and associated incidental works with work only disrupted when the engineers came under direct attack.

By October 1917, James and his comrades were working to the west of Ypres. Hours were long and the work was strenuous, often carried out in darkness or while under shell fire. Roads in the area were regularly targeted by enemy artillery and working parties were kept busy filling in the huge shell holes in an attempt to keep supply routes open. They dug new drainage ditches to replace those that had been destroyed, in a vain attempt to contain the watery mud that encompassed most of the battlefield and laid planks over the mud in the hope of producing a firmer road surface.

No matter how much effort the Field Companies put in, it was an ongoing battle. No sooner were roads repaired than they were shelled again. Every day, teams of engineers travelled out from their encampments to carry out repairs but frequently found it difficult or even impossible to make any progress. Ammunition wagons, and the many pack mules heading for the front line with water and supplies, struggled

---

[225] Nat Archives Ref WO 95/3129/4

to make progress through the mud and frequently created congestion, preventing the engineers from reaching their destination.

By December 1917 James's unit had moved into the ruined city of Ypres and was bivouacked east of the Menin Gate.[226] The men had been busy improving their dugouts when orders were issued to build a new Corps line. It was while he was involved in this work that James was wounded, and the incident is recorded in the war diary on 26th December: *"Parties shelled leaving work. 2 OR (L/Cpl [illegible] and Sapper Ray) wounded, one of whom died following day"*[227] The Register of Soldiers' Effects[228] confirms that the soldier who died was James. Further details are given in the Lijssenthoek visitor centre's web page.[229] James was taken to No3 Canadian Casualty Clearing Station where it was found that he had sustained severe injuries. These included a fractured spine and shrapnel wounds to his left side and abdomen. He died on the morning of 27th December 1917.

From April 1916, the 3rd Canadian CCS was located at Remy Siding, the largest evacuation hospital in the Ypres Salient, in the hamlet of Lijssenthoek. An adjacent railway line from Poperinghe facilitated the direct transfer of wounded from the battlefields. In addition, casualties who required advanced treatment further along the evacuation chain, or who were to be returned to England, could be loaded directly onto ambulance trains and transferred to base hospitals and evacuation quays near the coast. Transfers from Remy Siding were faster and more comfortable than the journey via horse-drawn or motorized ambulances faced by those at other medical units.

---

[226] Nat Archives Ref WO 95/3129/4
[227] Ibid
[228] Held at the National Army Museum and accessed through Ancestry
[229] lijssenthoek.be/en/page/160/visitor-centre.html

Over the years, a large cemetery grew up next to the medical unit at Remy Siding and this burial ground was later renamed Lijssenthoek Military Cemetery. It is now the second largest military cemetery in Belgium, with a total of 10,785 graves, 9901 of whom belong to British or Commonwealth troops. Only 24 of the graves remain unidentified. These were all concentrated into the cemetery at the end of the war, having been recovered from remote areas around Poperinghe.

James Ray was 22 years old when he was killed, and is buried in Plot XXVII.CC.1. In reporting his death, a Rossendale newspaper commented that he was *"an exceedingly promising young man and much esteemed by a large circle of friends and acquaintances."*[230] He is remembered on the war memorial at Holy Trinity Church, Tunstead and on the memorial stone in the Peace Garden at Newchurch Road, Stacksteads.

James Wray's Headstone at Lijssenthoek

---

[230] Rossendale Free Press: 5th January 1918

Chapter 11

Two events that occurred in 1917 were to have a decisive impact on the future course of the First World War. After Germany reintroduced unrestricted submarine warfare at the beginning of the year, US President Woodrow Wilson broke off diplomatic relations, citing Germany's action as a threat to the freedom of the seas. Hours later, the converted liner SS *Housatonic*, carrying a cargo of wheat and flour from Texas to Liverpool, was sunk off the Scilly Isles. After a number of other American vessels came under attack from U-boats while sailing in British waters, President Wilson made the decision to enter the war on the side of the Allies. Following his impassioned speech to congress, the Senate and House of Representatives gave their support and war was declared on 7th April 1917. On 26th June, the first 14,000 American troops arrived in France under the leadership of General Pershing. It was a "cobbled together Army"[231] of volunteers that still required many months of training before it would be ready to enter combat.

In 1917, the spotlight fell on political events in Russia. In February, large demonstrations against Tsar Nicholas II had begun in Petrograd. When the army refused to intervene and joined the revolt on the side of the demonstrators, Nicholas abdicated and the Romanov dynasty was replaced by a new provisional government under the leadership of Alexander Kerensky. Unpopular with the people because it failed to meet their demands for peace, it drew criticism from both the right and the left of politics. On 6th and 7th November, Bolsheviks led by Vladimir Lenin and Leon Trotsky

---

[231] www.army.mil/article/185229/ " Building the American Military" by Jim Garamone. April 3rd 2017

overthrew the provisional government and set up a Marxist state: the Russian Soviet Federative Socialist Republic. One of the new government's first decisions was to announce that the republic would immediately seek an armistice and withdraw from the war. On 3 March 1918, the Treaty of Brest-Litovsk was signed between Russia and the Central Powers, ending Russia's participation in hostilities.

Germany was quick to take advantage of the Russian withdrawal. As it was no longer faced with fighting a war on two fronts, some 50 German Divisions were transferred to the western front.[232] These were welcome reinforcements for troops who were depleted and exhausted by three years of fighting a war of attrition. Bolstered by their arrival, preparations were made for a final German offensive, in an attempt to bring the war to a successful conclusion before the Americans had time to mobilize their full resources and take an active part in the war.

The Allies had been entrenched in the same positions for months, dug in along a front line that stretched from the Somme to the Channel Coast. They were fully aware that an attack was in the offing, as aerial reconnaissance had reported the massive build-up of enemy forces. When the wind was in the right direction, in the stillness of the night, the continual rumble of enemy trains and transport could be heard bringing many thousands of German soldiers and heavy equipment forward. In dire need of reinforcements themselves, the British were strung out thinly along the length of the front. Morale was low and they knew that they were about to face a major German attack for the first time in three years. The only question was: when would it happen?

The German Spring Offensive was launched on 21st March 1918. The plan was to break through the front quickly

---

[232] A German WW1 Division in 1914 was 18,000 men but this had reduced to around 15,000 later in the war

in a number of places and overwhelm the Allies with the strength and momentum of the German attack. They would then force their way through to the Channel ports, capturing the main railheads at Arras and Amiens on the way. This would ensure that British supply routes were blocked and force the Allies into defeat.

The attack began with an enormous artillery barrage along the entire 40 mile front, "*a terrific bombardment. . . which heralded the opening of the mightiest attack in the history of warfare.*"[233] The British were stunned by the speed and ferocity of the attack. By the end of the first day their casualties amounted to 7,512 dead and 10,000 wounded, the 5th Army had been pushed back 9 miles and 21,000 allied soldiers had been taken prisoner.

The Germans continued to advance, forcing the British 5th Army to retreat back over the Somme ground they had fought so hard to win in 1916. German success continued, and by 5th April they had advanced 40 miles into British territory and captured 70,000 prisoners and 1000 British guns.

Although the German Spring Offensive began on the Somme, a second attack, the Battle of the Lys, began in Flanders on 7th April. The objective was to capture the town of Ypres, now in complete ruin, which the British had held since they drove out the Germans in October 1914. If Ypres could be taken, the British would be forced back to the Channel ports, their supply routes would be cut and they would ultimately be forced out of the war.

The Battle, also known as the Fourth Battle of Ypres, was fought between 7th and 29th April. It consisted of a number of different German attacks, and among their forces were members of the new highly-trained Stormtrooper unit, skilled in infiltration tactics that would be used to good effect when

---

[233] History of the 42nd Division by Frederick P Gibbon

storming British trenches. Against them was the British First Army. Weary and short of men, it had been transferred to this "quiet area" to allow the troops to recover from previous engagements.

German troops managed to advance about 10 miles into British held territory, but they failed in their aim to capture Ypres. French reinforcements arrived in the area towards the end of April and, having suffered many casualties without gaining their objective, the German High Command called off the attack. Britain suffered around 82,000 casualties during the Spring attacks; a similar number was recorded by Germany.

British Troops Blinded By Gas in 1918 [234]

---

[234] By kind permission of the Keasbury-Gordon Photograph Archive

Captain Norman Wilkinson
9th Battalion, Manchester Regiment
Died 21st March 1918

Remembered
Pozières Memorial

Norman Wilkinson,[235] second child and eldest son of Bessie and Fred Wilkinson, was born at 12 Park Street, Haslingden on the 17th February 1889. He first attended the town's Wesley Elementary School, where his father was the Headmaster, before he was admitted to NGS on 2nd May 1899. A high-performing student, he won an All-England Scholarship to Christ's Hospital School in Horsham where he joined the cadet corps.

He began his medical studies at Owen's College, University of Manchester in 1907 and also joined the local Volunteers, where he served as a driver in the transport section of the Royal Army Medical Corps (RAMC). Volunteers, along with Militia and Yeomanry, augmented the

---

[235] Photograph: Rossendale Free Press 18 May 1918

Army's Home Service in a part-time capacity but by the time the Volunteers became part of the Territorial Force under the 1908 Haldane Army Reforms, Norman had reached the end of his period of service and was discharged. In his university vacations, he spent time at the home of the Surgeon James Atkinson in Crewe, learning from and assisting the surgeon in his work.[236]

Norman's service record is on file at the National Archives[237] and this shows that he joined up on 26th September 1914. His school cadet training stood him in good stead as he secured a commission immediately. Gazetted on 12th October, he joined the 9th battalion, Manchester Regiment as a 2nd Lieutenant.[238] Promotion came quickly, to temporary Lieutenant in November 1914 and then to temporary Captain in June 1915.[239] The temporary prefix was used to identify officers who had enlisted for the duration of the war, rather than joining the regular army. His early military service appears to have included periods fighting in France and Flanders, but there is nothing in his records to say when he went overseas or where he served at that time.

Later posted as adjutant to the 1/8th (Irish) battalion of the King's Liverpool Regiment, he developed trench fever while serving in France with them and was evacuated from Boulogne on 22nd January 1917 aboard the hospital ship HMS *Dieppe*. Admitted to 3rd Australian General Hospital in Brighton, his recovery was slow. On 2nd July he was examined by a medical board and considered still to be unfit for service overseas.

---

[236] https://hasligdenwarheroes.blogspot.com for N Wilkinson
[237] National Archives reference WO 374/74513
[238] Supplement to the London Gazette 13th November 1914, page 9276
[239] Supplement to the London Gazette dated 17 August 1915, page 8253

While based in England, Norman completed a training course at bombing school. This was followed by a posting as Temporary Captain attached to the 2/4th Norfolk Regiment, who were engaged in east coast defence work. On 14th July 1917, he was finally passed fit for General Service and was recalled to France. He embarked at the end of July and, after a spell with the 2/8th Manchester Regiment, was posted to the 1/9th Battalion and put in command of B Company. Shortly afterwards, the battalion was ordered into the Ypres sector and remained there until the end of the year.

At the beginning of December 1917, Norman went home for what was to be his last leave. He spent almost two weeks in Haslingden and arrived back at his unit just before Christmas. Shortly after his return, the battalion was ordered back to the Somme and Norman was given the post of Transport Officer.

In January 1918 troops learned that a huge reorganisation of British forces was underway. The army had a manpower crisis and was struggling to bring battalions up to fighting strength. The only way that this could be done was to cut the number of battalions and distribute the men among those that remained. They would be more thinly spread out along the front, but each unit would be up to strength. Under these plans, the 1/9th battalion was absorbed into the 2/9th and the resultant unit was renamed the 9th battalion.

When the German Spring Offensive began on 21st March, the 9th Battalion was entrenched on the Somme about 8 miles east of Peronne. Under attack from before dawn, they were bombarded by gas shells and suffered heavy casualties. Norman died on the first day of the attack. He was 29 years old.

Shortly after his son's death, Fred Wilkinson received a letter from the Battalion Commander in which he explained that Norman had been killed by a shell and had died instantly. He said he had been a *"sterling fellow"* who would be a tremendous loss. Lt Colonel Heselton[240] also wrote to Mr Wilkinson. He related how Norman had often passed time in the mess with another of his (the Lt Col's) late officers, Captain Wright.[241] He wrote, *"Both are now dead. . . thank God that England breeds such boys!"* [242]

The war diary for the period 21st- 30th March appears to have been written up after the first phase of the attack ended on 1st April; this is quite understandable, considering that the whole British army was in full retreat during this period. A brief note covers the last 10 days of the month and noted *"during the time from 21st/31st March the battalion was continuously in action and fought very hard."*[243] The 9th battalion's casualties for the period are listed; 25 officers and 630 other ranks killed, wounded or missing. Of the officers, six were known to have been killed and three were missing.

The local newspaper account of Norman's death noted that his father was waiting for more new about the circumstances of his son's death as there were said to be *"slight discrepancies."* There is nothing to say what these were but an official form in Norman's file may throw some light on the matter. At the end of the war, the government announced that the next of kin of those who had died were to receive a plaque and scroll as "a memorial of their patriotism and sacrifice." [244] In July 1919, when returning the acceptance letter to the War Office, Fred Wilkinson wrote the following in the margin: *"Is it possible for me to ascertain whether or no (sic) my son was buried and if so, where?"*[245] There is nothing in

---

[240] Lt Col J L Heselton
[241] Edward M Wright is also remembered on the Roll of Honour at BRGS
[242] https://hasligdenwarheroes.blogspot.com – N Wilkinson
[243] National Archives Ref WO 95/3145/5
[244] These are often referred to as 'Death Pennies' or 'Dead Man's Penny'
[245] National Archive Ref WO 374/74513

the file to indicate whether this request was ever answered but Norman has no known grave.

Norman Wilkinson's name is engraved along with 499 of his regimental comrades on panels 64 to 67 of the Pozières Memorial on the Somme. The memorial surrounds Pozières British Cemetery on three sides and commemorates over 14,000 United Kingdom and 300 South African forces who have no known grave and who died in the area between the 21st March and 7th August 1918. His name is inscribed on the Haslingden Memorial Roll, which now hangs in the stairwell at Haslingden Public Library, and on the World War 1 Memorials at Manchester University and Christ's Hospital School.

Entrance to Pozières
Cemetery & Memorial

Lance Corporal Albert John Holt
2/5th Battalion, East Lancashire Regiment
Died 31st March 1918

Remembered
Pozières Memorial

Born on 20th November 1894, Albert was the fourth and youngest child of Joseph and Jemima Holt. Joseph was a journeyman joiner and the family lived at 94 Burnley Road in Waterfoot. Albert received his formative education at Newchurch National School and then transferred to Newchurch Grammar School on 15th January 1907. After he left school he entered the slipper trade, working as an office boy at H W Trickett Ltd in Waterfoot.

Albert served as 241827 Lance Corporal Holt in the 2/5th Battalion, East Lancashire Regiment. Raised at Burnley in 1914, the 2/5th served as a home service unit, providing replacement drafts for the service battalion and responsible for home defence. As casualties mounted on the Western Front, the manpower shortage became more severe and home service units were called up for active service. The 2/5th East Lancs was sent to France in March 1917 as part of these replacements, and entries in the war diary for the months immediately after they landed in France provide a picture of what life at the front was like for Albert and his comrades.[246] The handwriting in this diary, in contrast to that of many others, is very clear. Although the entries are concise, the writer included useful background details in addition to the more normal information relating to troop movements, operations and casualties. Unfortunately, because his service record is one of those that did not survive the London Blitz, it is impossible to know whether Albert joined the battalion while they were in England or after they had arrived in France.

An advance party of the battalion left the Regimental barracks at Colchester on 10th February 1917 and was followed a few weeks later by a first line transport section which disembarked at Le Havre on 2nd March. The battalion's remaining personnel travelled from Colchester via Folkestone and embarked for Boulogne on the SS *'Invicta'* on 4th March 1917. After resting and receiving reserve rations, they journeyed by train to the 66th Division concentration area at Thiennes, north west of Bethune. A few officers and men went straight from there into the trenches, while others joined working parties and salvage companies before being ordered into the line.

The months that followed were fairly quiet, and their work appears to have fallen into a regular pattern. When in the front line, the soldiers went out on trench raids and night patrols, shored up and repaired damaged trenches and carried out harrying tactics such as exploding mines in enemy territory. When relieved, they fell back to spend time in the support trenches before they went into the reserve line.

---

[246] National Archives Ref WO 95/3141/5

Time away from the trenches was spent in billets or camps behind the lines and troops were kept fully occupied. They received regular musketry and bayonet practice, rehearsed and perfected attack skills, attended church services, held concerts and took part in inter-company and inter-regimental sports matches. Good hygiene was known to boost morale, and time in billets was used for baths and cleaning uniforms and equipment.

As the war progressed, time spent in the trenches increased and delousing sessions, carried out under regimental orders, became an absolute necessity. Casualties still occurred during these quieter periods but, according to the diary, these were fairly light, and sickness and accidents took a greater toll. Moved to the Dunkirk area in June 1917, the battalion operated along the Flanders coast. Training sessions were increased and the East Lancs men joined the Royal Engineers in a special exercise which involved 'boating and bridge building.'[247]

In September 1917, the battalion moved to the east of Ypres, where they were to take part in the Battle of Poelcappelle.[248] The battalion commenced their attack on enemy positions at 5.20am on 9th October. By the end of that day, they had achieved their objective, with only light casualties, and held their position in the line until they were relieved. Only then were they organised into working parties and sent out to gather in the wounded and bury their dead.

Over the following months, Albert's battalion were continually in and out of the line, moving position as headquarters dictated. With the approach of winter, the front had quietened down and Christmas Day was decreed a holiday. By March of 1918, they had left the sea of mud that

---

[247] National Archives Reference WO 95/3141/5
[248] A phase of Third Battle of Ypres. The entire campaign is more commonly referred to as Passchendaele

was the Flanders' battlefield and had returned to France, where they were in position at Hargicourt on the Aisne.

This period of relative calm came to an abrupt end on 21st March when the Germans launched their massive attack over a narrow front. With overwhelming firepower and following numerous gas attacks they penetrated and held many British forward positions. This resulted in a high casualty rate and widespread confusion among the British troops. With their battalion headquarters outflanked, the 2/5th East Lancs withdrew at 1pm and dug in at their new positions in the rear. Unable to hold the line, they were forced into retreat and by 23rd March had been pushed back as far as Peronne. Here they came to a halt with orders to guard the bridgehead and cover the mass British withdrawal.

At 8am on 25th March, four days after the Spring Offensive began, the Germans attacked the East Lancs in their new positions and, despite valiant attempts to repulse them over many hours, the battalion had to withdraw under cover of darkness; first to Foucaucourt and then to Hamel. On receiving orders to halt their retreat there, the 2/5th battalion took up a defensive position and held it until they were outflanked yet again and forced back even further. This continual rear-guard cat and mouse action continued until 31st March, by which time the battalion had reached Hanguard, about 10 miles south east of Amiens. Here they dug in and managed to hold their position until they were relieved on 2nd April.

Much of the ground won during five months of fighting on the Somme in 1916 had been lost to the enemy in less than two weeks. On 1st March, the 2/5th battalion's fighting strength had been 52 officers and 922 men[249] but at roll call on the 31st, only 11 officers were still fit for service. Casualties

---

[249] National Archives Ref WO 95/3141/5

for all other ranks totalled 43 killed, 124 wounded and 563 missing.

Albert was killed on 31st March while the battalion were fighting a rear-guard action. He was 24 years old. As he has no known grave, his name is inscribed on the Pozières Memorial on the Somme. At home in Rossendale he is remembered on the WW1 plaque in St Nicholas Church, Newchurch and at the Trickett's Memorial Ground in Waterfoot. This memorial takes the form of two plaques mounted on the gate pillars of a small memorial garden on Burnley Road East, Waterfoot. The land was purchased and presented to the local community by the firm of Sir H W Trickett Ltd, the local slipper manufacturing company for whom Albert worked and whose staff raised funds to remember all 44 of their former colleagues who fell in the Great War.

Trickett's Memorial Ground

Private Michael Heys
12th Battalion, Royal Scots
Died 22nd April 1918

Haringhe (Bandaghem)
Military Cemetery

Searching for background information on Michael Heys was a difficult task. Admission records at NGS contained the information that he was born in Rawtenstall on 5th March 1883 but gave no parental details. An internet search found a copy of his obituary from a local newspaper, but no date was attached to the entry.[250] This report included the information that Michael had a brother and two sisters, and that he was the son of the late John Heys, former owner of a Bacup cycle shop. Both Michael's parents had died by the time this obituary was written.

An examination of census records shows a complicated family background. In 1891, 8-year-old Michael was living at

---

[250] The undated clipping was found in the 1918 section of the website www.bacuptimes.co.uk

15 Elm Street in Newchurch with his widowed grandmother, Mary Edwards, and her five grown up children. There was no mention of his siblings. NGS admission records indicate that Michael's early education began at Thorn Chapel School in Bacup. The school was run under the auspices of Mount Pleasant Wesleyan Church and was originally known as the 'Chapel for the Destitute' or the 'Ragged School.' Rebuilt on a new site in 1872, it was renamed Thorn Chapel. Michael appears to have applied himself to his studies, as he went up to Newchurch Grammar School in February 1896 as a 'Lawfield Scholar'.[251]

1901 census records show that Michael was employed as a slipper heel builder and was living at 79 Todmorden Road in Bacup with his great aunt, Mary Maybury, and another two of her great-nephews and two great-nieces. One of the males, John R Heys, was four years older than Michael and worked as a slipper finisher. Information found in later documents proved that John was Michael's elder brother. The other three children in the house were all under seven, although they also had the surname Heys. By the date of the 1911 census, Michael and John had moved away from Rossendale and were lodging together at 7 Hanson Street in Bury, the home of shoe finishers William and Sarah Nuttall.

A service record for a Michael Heys survives at the National Archives. This file was initially discounted as the Attestation Form showed the soldier's place of birth to be Dundee. When no trace of any other Michael Heys was found in any military records, the papers at the National Archives were scrutinised more closely. The year of birth and occupation matched those of Rawtenstall-born Michael and the next of kin was given a brother, John R Heys. A search of the 'Scotland's People' genealogical website[252] found that no

---

[251] No information has been found relating to this scholarship
[252] scotlandspeople.gov.uk

one with the name Michael Heys had been registered anywhere in Scotland between the years 1855 and 1918. On this evidence it appears that 'Dundee' was an error[253] made by the clerk completing Michael's Attestation Letter at the recruiting centre and that the record at Kew, for a Private Michael Heys of the Royal Scots, is indeed that of the former Newchurch Grammar School pupil.

The file also provided the information that before he joined up Michael was living with his brother John at 149 North Road in Longsight. He enlisted at Manchester on 24th August 1915 and, as Private 27231, joined the 18th Battalion of the Royal Scots, the regiment's training battalion, before he went to France on 12th February 1916. He continued to train at one of the Army base camps located around Étaples, while he waited to be posted to a Service unit. On 23rd May he joined the 15th battalion, Royal Scots Regiment.

Michael's file includes his medical record, which shows that he was wounded on three separate occasions while in France. On 9th April 1917, the first day of the Battle of Arras, he was shot in his left shoulder. Initially treated by the 103rd Field Ambulance (FA), he was taken to General Hospital 4 near Étaples and then evacuated back to England on the Belgian owned HS *Stad Antwerpen*. On arrival in England on 27th April, he was admitted to The Cambridge Hospital in Aldershot. He went back out to France on 11th June and was posted to D Company of the Regiment's 12th Battalion on 29th June.

When Michael next returned home on leave, he married Miss Rosa Marie Henson on 24th November 1917. Shortly after their marriage, he returned to the front and was wounded again, on 11th December. He was admitted to the 27th Field Ambulance Station the following day with gun-shot

---

[253] It is not uncommon for similar errors to be found, possibly due to the volume of paperwork clerks had to process throughout the war.

wounds to his right armpit and right thigh. Initially sent to 5th Casualty Clearing Station (CCS), he was transferred to hospital at Étaples and on 6th January 1918 was moved to the larger Base Hospital at Trouville. He returned to his battalion in early March but was wounded again on 18th April. Shot in both legs, he was taken to the 63rd CCS where he died.

The war diaries of the 12th and 15th battalions detail their movements around the dates when Michael was wounded. On the first occasion, in April 1917, the 15th Battalion had left their billets at Arras and moved into trenches in readiness for an attack. Conditions were difficult. The weather was very wet and, while the troops were digging-in, their trenches were regularly shelled.

The British assault began at 5.30am on 9th April and Michael's battalion moved forward in support around 7.30am. The diarist noted that, since their numbers were depleted following recent artillery bombardments, the troops had to move forward in a thin line. With British guns at their maximum range, the covering artillery barrage was lighter than had been expected. When the battalion had almost reached their objective, they were faced with enemy field guns firing shrapnel shells at almost point blank range. This was followed by intense rifle fire. These two attacks left fifty men dead and injured.

Although they met with considerable resistance, the 15th Royal Scots achieved their primary objective and were able to hold the line, but after an enemy counter-attack later in the day, the decision was made to postpone any further advance.

In April 1918, while serving with the Regiment's 12th battalion, Michael received the wounds which ultimately led to his death. The 12th Royal Scots were in position around Kemmel, about 7 miles south east of the town of Poperinghe in Belgium. The soldiers were attempting to repulse a German attack on Kemmel Ridge and the fierce fighting resulted in very heavy casualties on both sides. The British managed to repulse the attack. The bravery of the 12th Royal Scots is perhaps best illustrated by the number of gallantry medals awarded to the battalion at the end of April; 4 Distinguished Conduct Medals, 4 Military Crosses, 8 Military Medals and a bar to a previously awarded Distinguished Service Order.

The Battle of Kemmel, part of the Battle of the Lys,[254] was fought between 17th and 19th April 1918. The Germans attacked the ridge known as the Kemmelberg and Michael's battalion, as part of the 9th Division, were ordered to resist the attack. Michael was wounded around this time, most likely during the events described above, although there is nothing in his record or in the war diary to say exactly where or when it occurred. Neither are there any details of when he entered the medical evacuation train.

In the first instance he would have been treated at an Aid Post or Field Ambulance before he was moved further away from the front, back towards the nearest Casualty Clearing Station. His service record includes a Field Service Form (Army Form B2090a) and this clearly shows that he was admitted to No 63 CCS, where he died of his wounds on 22nd April 1918. He was buried in the cemetery at Bandaghem which grew up next to No 62 and No 63 CCS. The cemetery is now known as Haringhe[255] Military Cemetery and Michael lies in plot III.E.32. Aged 35 when he died, he was one of the oldest NGS boys to die in the Great War.

Today, cemeteries that grew up around Casualty Clearing Stations can be identified by the way many of the headstones are packed tightly together in chronological order. After a major attack, medical units were inundated with casualties,

---

[254] Also known as the fourth Battle of Ypres
[255] During the war this area near the town of Poperinghe was known as Bandaghem.

many of whom did not survive their injuries. Due to the large numbers involved, it was impractical to dig individual graves and so the men were laid to rest in long trenches. The headstones erected by the CWGC after the war show the location of the trench burial but in many cases do not mark the exact location of the individual.

Grave of Michael Heys
Haringhe (Bandaghem) Military Cemetery

Sapper James Greenwood Collinge
33rd Light Railway Company, Royal Engineers
Died 25th April 1918

Nine Elms British Cemetery
Poperinghe, Belgium

James was the youngest of seven children. Born to James and Sarah Collinge in Stacksteads, Lancashire on 9th January 1896, he lived at 198 Newchurch Road. The 1901 census shows that his father ran his own grocer's shop. Young James attended St Saviour's Elementary School and joined Newchurch Grammar School on 19th January 1909. When he left school he worked as an assistant in his father's grocery shop and later worked as a clerk at the Lancashire & Yorkshire Railway Company's Goods Station at Bacup. Following his death, the local newspaper reported that Mr Rhodes, the Superintendent of the Goods Department and carting agent Mr J Seed both remembered James as a most efficient and estimable young man.[256]

James Collinge enlisted at Rawtenstall on 5th May 1915, aged 19, and was issued with service number L18031. He was assigned to the Royal Field Artillery (RFA) as a Driver and joined D Company, 170th County Palatine Brigade at Lytham. On 1st June he was appointed as an assistant bomber and trained at Lytham, Blackpool and on Salisbury Plain. Later promoted to the full rank of bombardier, he sailed from Devonport on 8th December 1915 and landed at Port Said on 22nd of the month. After serving in Egypt for around two months, James's unit sailed from Alexandria on 3rd March 1916 and arrived at Marseilles a week later. He travelled up though France with them and joined the British Expeditionary Force (BEF) on the Western Front.

James's service record survives at the National Archives[257] and this shows that he requested a transfer to the Royal Engineers. As he had been a railway worker in peacetime, his skills were put to good use and he worked as a guard in the Railway Transport Department at Boulogne from 23rd February 1917. On 12th April he was transferred to the 33rd Light Railway Company, still as a guard, and was issued with a new service number, 252021. A promotion from Sapper to 2nd Corporal followed on 1st April 1918.

Before the introduction of Light Railway Companies, the British Army had used normal gauge railway tracks and rolling stock to move equipment, ammunition and troops from the Channel ports to divisional railheads. From there, they were dependent on horse transport to reach the front lines. As it became more and more difficult to keep and maintain clear roads, supplies and amunition bound for the front were often delayed and men heading for the front often

---

[256] Rossendale Free Press: 4th May 1918
[257] Service Record for James Greenwood is available at Ancestry

had to march long distances from the railhead to reach their positions. The introduction of narrow gauge railways. light and easily assembled exactly where they were needed, enabled men and munitions to be transported more quickly. Each Light Railway Company (LRC) consisted of 200 men who carried out a variety of jobs associated with rail transport, from drivers, guards and engineers to storesmen, stock repairers and warehousemen.

James service record shows that he died of wounds on 25th April 1918, but there is nothing to indicate how or where he was injured. An internet search found an old enquiry on the Great War Forum.[258] A subscriber wrote that, following a visit to Nine Elms Cemetery near Poperinghe, *"I came across a line of Royal Engineers who died on the same day, 25th April 1918. Some were in the 33rd Light Railway Coy,....does anyone have further details about their deaths?"*[259] Another forum member replied to the post saying that he had found a newspaper obituary for one of the men, James Collinge, in a local newspaper. This detailed how his parents had learned of their son's death from one of his friends, 2nd Corporal J Anderson,[260] who had been in the same working party. He explained that six men had been killed and several seriously injured.

A further internet search found a service record for 251901, 2/Cpl Robert Birse who had also served with the 33rd LRC and who died on the same day as James Collinge. Among his papers at the National Archives was a copy of a telegram sent to the Royal Engineers Records Office in London from 140th Field Ambulance.[261] The telegram reported that there had been four deaths at the unit on 25th April 1918, all from 33rd Light Railway Company, and listed

---

[258] greatwarforum.org
[259] greatwarforum.org/forums - 33rd Light Railway Engineering Company
[260] 2nd Corporal was a WW1 RE rank
[261] Service Record for Robert Birse accessed through Ancestry

their names. One of the casualties was named as 2/Cpl J G Collinge who had been admitted with gunshot wounds to his head, hand and leg.[262] At that date 140th Field Ambulance were located at Brandhoek, a village midway between Poperinghe and Ypres.[263]

The date of the men's injuries coincided with the German attack on the Kemmelberg on 25th and 26th April. On the night before, as a precursor to the attack, the Germans had bombarded the British lines for hours. The 140th Field Ambulance's diary for the night of the 24th reported artillery fire in and around Kemmel, south of their position at Brandhoek. The diary shows that during the night of 24th April, "*the railway yard came under heavy shelling resulting in several casualties with four dead and twenty wounded brought in.*" [264]

Sarah Collinge made repeated efforts to have her son's personal effects returned to her, and a number of her letters are in the service record.[265] In a letter dated 29th May which she sent to the Transportation Department at Tavistock Square in London, she gave more information about the circumstances of James's death. In writing for an explanation as to why, "other than Army protocol", her son's possessions could not be returned to her more quickly, Sarah wrote that at the time he was wounded, her son had been working in the railway yard behind the lines. She had been informed that he had been carried unconscious from the scene by "*RAMC men*" but had died before reaching the field hospital.[266]

---

[262] Service Record for Robert Birse at Ancestry
[263] The Long Long Trail - longlongtrail.co.uk army/regiments-and-corps/locations-of-british-casualty-clearing-stations
[264] National Archives Ref Wo 95/2630/1
[265] Service Record accessed through Ancestry
[266] Information received from her son's friend, Corporal J Anderson

James is buried in Plot XIV.C.5 at Nine Elms British Cemetery, located a few miles to the west of Poperinghe in Belgium. He is remembered on the memorial stone in the Peace Garden at Stacksteads and on the Lancashire and Yorkshire Railway's War Memorial at the main entrance to Victoria Station, Manchester. Nine days after his death, the Rossendale Free Press reported his death and noted that *"several letters have been received from pals expressing their deep regret at having lost such a good and fine chum."*[267]

Nine Elms Cemetery near Poperinghe

---

[267] Rossendale Free Press: 4th May 1918

Gunner Willie Rae Walker Pickup
Royal Garrison Artillery
Died 3rd May 1918

Eastern Cemetery
Boulogne, France

Early life for Willie Rae Pickup[268] was very different from that of the other men from NGS who died in the Great War. He was born and spent his early years in the United States. His father, John Wimpenny Pickup, went to America in 1891 where he met Michigan-born Phoebe Bailey. The couple married in Pennsylvania in 1892 and Willie Rae Walker Pickup, known to the family as Rae, was born in Philadelphia on 18th November in the same year. His brother was born eighteen months later.

Rae Pickup attended the Central High School of Philadelphia, but after Phoebe died from typhoid in 1906,[269] John returned to England with his two sons. The NGS admission records at BRGS show that both boys were

---

[268] Photograph: Bacup Times 11 May 1918
[269] www.genealogy.com/forum/surnames/topics/pickup/84/

admitted to the school on 14th October 1907 and that at that time they were living with their father, an unemployed cotton manufacturer, at Spring Villa, New Line in Bacup. This was the family home in which John had been brought up in the years before he went to America.

Census data shows that eighteen-year-old Rae had finished his education and was working as an articled civil engineer in Bacup Corporation's Engineering Department in 1911. His father had remarried in 1909 and the family still lived at Spring Villa, where they employed a young servant girl, twenty-year-old Florence Holbrooke. On 20th December 1913, Rae and Florence married at Haslingden Register Office and the couple set up home at 24 Ribble Street in Bacup. In later years, this was where they brought up their two young daughters. When he finished his professional exams, Rae began working as an assistant surveyor with Bacup Council.

Rae's service record is at the National Archives and confirms that he enlisted on 11th December 1915. Gunner 97766 Pickup was mobilized on 7th June 1916 and travelled to 2 Depot, Royal Garrison Artillery (RGA), where he joined 151 Heavy Battery.[270] He embarked with his battery on 19th June 1916, but shortly after his arrival in France, Rae was transferred to the 22nd Heavy Battery. He passed his signalling test on 1st September and was reclassified as a Signaller 1st Class.

RGA Heavy Batteries were located well behind the front line. They were equipped with large guns and howitzers that fired explosive shells over long distances. Observers closer to the front communicated with signallers like Rae in order to direct the guns onto enemy positions. Heavy artillery was used to eliminate or damage enemy artillery, destroy

---

[270] The guns of the Army's heavy batteries were positioned far behind the line and had immense destructive power.

ammunition dumps and stores and disrupt communication and supply lines. As a consequence, gun teams regularly came under heavy, retaliatory artillery fire and casualties among gun teams were commonplace.

Rae's casualty report is in his file. He was wounded on 1st October 1917 and admitted to the 1st Australian General Hospital at Rouen six days later. On 20th November, his medical notes were updated to show 'Shell Shock'. He returned to Lancashire on furlough the following January and spent ten days at home before he returned to the front.

On Sunday 5th May 1918, a sister at the 13th General Hospital at Boulogne sent a card to Florence advising her Rae had been admitted to hospital after a gas attack but that his condition wasn't serious. On the same day, she received a telegram notifying her that her husband was now dangerously ill. The last entry in Rae's medical record is dated 4th May. It is a report written by the officer in command of the 13th General Hospital and states that Gunner Pickup had died from 'gas shell wounds' on 3rd May, two days before the letter and telegram were received by his wife in Bacup. The week before his death he had written to his wife confirming that he was *"with the best of health."*[271]

The 13th General Hospital in Boulogne was one of the most important base hospitals on the Western Front and was used extensively by allied forces during the war. Casualties tended to be evacuated to Northern base hospitals for more advanced and specialist care and the units were typically staffed by older, more senior doctors than those nearer the front. Despite this advanced care, Rae failed to recover from his injuries. He was 25 years old when he died.

Rae Pickup is remembered on the Bacup War Memorial and at the family church, St Saviour's, New Line, Bacup. His

---

[271] Bacup Times: 11th May 1918

death was reported in the Bacup Times under the heading 'Promising Career Closed' and continued *"A finely set up young man, he had every promise of a successful career and his death will be greatly deplored."*[272] He is buried in Boulogne's Eastern Cemetery at Plot IX.B.3. Visitors will notice the cemetery is very different in appearance from the majority of CWGC cemeteries in France and Belgium. Due to the soft, sandy soil in the area all the headstones lie flat on the ground. They are rectangular in shape and do not have the characteristic curved top that so often denotes a CWGC grave.

Eastern Cemetery Boulogne-sur-Mer

---

[272] Bacup Times: 11th May 1918

2nd Lieutenant Norman Whittaker
3rd Battalion, King's Own Lancaster Regiment
Died 12th May 1918

Lapugnoy Military Cemetery
Bethune

Norman Whittaker was born on 1st May 1887. He was the only son of James Whittaker, chief mechanic at a local slipper factory, and his wife, Grace. After first attending Newchurch National School, he was enrolled at Newchurch Grammar School on 15th September 1897. He left school in December 1903, having "met with a good measure of success,"[273] and started work as a clerk at the Waterfoot branch of the Lancashire and Yorkshire Bank. In his youth, Norman was a member of St James' Church and Sunday School in Waterfoot, where he was a lay preacher, Sunday School teacher and member of the church choir. He was also Clerk to the Church Wardens and Secretary of the Church Benefit

---

[273] Bacup Times: 18 May 1918

Society. On hearing of his death, the vicar of St James' said he had been *"a young man of exceptional promise and one whom the church could ill afford to lose."*[274] Norman married Alberta Braddock on 31st August 1915 and the couple began their married life at 6 St James Street in Waterfoot.

During the war, local newspapers carried lists of casualties and often included personal and regimental details. An obituary for Norman was found in the archives of both the Rossendale Free Press[275] and the Lancashire Daily Post.[276] Each reported that 2nd Lieutenant N Whitaker, son of Mrs & Mrs J E Whittaker of Waterfoot, had been killed in action on 12th May 1918. The Rossendale Free Press confirmed that had been a pupil at NGS.

Since no regimental details were included in the newspaper report, a search of the CWGC online database was carried out. This found six possible WW1 matches; two for 'Norman Whittaker' and four for 'N Whittaker. Of these, only one man was listed as an officer, a 2nd Lt N Whittaker of the King's Own Royal Lancaster Regiment. He had been killed on 12th May 1918 which corresponded with the information in the newspaper report. The correct man had been identified.

A search at the National Archives discovered a file for Norman among the Officer Long Number Papers.[277] He enlisted on 9th December 1915 and joined the 3rd battalion of the East Lancashire Regiment. Issued with service number 23598, he was posted to the Reserve. Mobilized on 12th June 1916, he joined the 12th East Lancashire Regiment for initial training.[278]

---

[274] Bacup Times: 18th May 1918
[275] Ibid
[276] Lancashire Daily Post: 30th May 1918
[277] National Archives Ref WO 339/94132
[278] This was the Reserve Battalion for the Accrington Pals

In the early months of the war, recruitment surged to such an extent that volunteers were often posted to a regiment's reserve battalion until a space became available at a training establishment. As numbers of new recruits fell away during 1915, the time between enlistment and the start of training tended to decrease. With the introduction of conscription at the beginning of 1916, recruitment increased so dramatically that individual regiments simply could not cope with the number of men they were expected to train. To speed up the induction process, the system where individual regiments carried out training was abandoned in favour of a new training system. Introduced in August 1916, the Training Reserve was to be responsible for all training. The 12th East Lancashire battalion, to which Norman had been posted, was re-designated 75th Training Reserve Battalion (TRB) and at that point broke all links with the East Lancashire regiment.

The 75th TRB, based at Prees Heath in Shropshire, was responsible for training some 30,000 soldiers at a time. Norman completed his training on 1st September, after which he was sent to the 12th Liverpool (Service) Battalion and received the new service number 56136. He embarked for France on 26th September and, after a few days at a Base Depot near the coast, joined his battalion on the Somme. He appears to have shown early promise, as he was promoted to Lance Corporal on 3rd November 1916, a short time after he arrived at the front.

His sound work ethic attracted the attention of senior officers who recommended him for a commission.[279] He left France for cadet school[280] at Seaforth near Liverpool in January 1917 and began his officers' training at Lichfield. On 27th July, he joined the 3rd (Reserve) Battalion of the King's

---

[279] National Archives Ref WO 339/94132
[280] From 1916, prospective officers had to pass out from cadet school before they could begin their officer training

Own Royal Lancaster Regiment (KORLR) with the rank of 2nd Lieutenant. Posted back to France, he was attached to the Regiment's 1/4th battalion shortly after he arrived and joined his new unit on the 18th August.

The battalion spent the rest of August undergoing training behind the lines in preparation for a move into Belgium in early September. The Third Battle of Ypres had begun on 31st July and the battalion was ordered to move up as reinforcements. The day after their arrival on the Salient they were attacked from the air and a number of soldiers were killed. A repeat attack on the 16th September killed a further three men.

Norman was wounded in this second attack when he was hit in the left arm by an anti-aircraft machine gun bullet. He was sent to the Red Cross Base Hospital at Rouen where the wound was considered serious enough for him to be sent home to England. He arrived at the 4th Southern General Hospital in Plymouth on 23rd September and a month later, was moved to an officers' convalescent home at Sutton Coldfield. By January 1918, he had recovered and was given 3 weeks' leave before he returned to the front for a third time.

2Lt Whittaker arrived at the British army's main Infantry Base Depot (IBD)[281] on 17th April and was posted on attachment to the KORLR's 1st battalion. The unit war diary for on 24th April noted his arrival while they were in camp near the village of Cense La Vallee near Bethune. After a quiet few days behind the lines, the unit were ordered forward and came under heavy enemy artillery fire during the night of 28th April. The next evening, under cover of darkness, various working parties were sent out to bury the battalion's dead, salvage equipment and repair the wire in

---

[281] Positioned near the Channel ports and receiving men coming out from England, the IBDs were responsible for maintaining soldiers' training while they waiting to be posted to the Front.

their forward positions. A few days later they withdrew from the front line and returned to Brigade Reserve. On 12th May, a simple one line entry in the diary stated "*2/Lieut N Whittaker K in Action*"[282] He was 31 years old and, although the diary gives no indication of how Norman died, it does recount an incident that may explain what happened.

An appendix to the diary entries for the month of May reported that while they were in the line, the sector held by the 1st battalion had been "fairly quiet", with the exception of the area around Canal Bank. This was a reference to the La Bassée canal, which had been heavily targeted by the enemy with both high explosive and gas shells. When the 1st Battalion were relieved and moved from Canal Bank into Brigade Reserve, one company of the battalion was ordered to remain behind at Canal Bank. With only limited information in the diary, it is impossible to positively identify which officer led the company that remained behind, but with the remainder of the battalion in Brigade Reserve on the date Norman died, it is possible he was killed while defending the position.

According to the local newspaper report of his death, Norman wrote home regularly and his letters were always bright and cheery. His wife had received a letter from him on 15th May in which he'd told her all was well. He had mentioned that he was 'going up the line' but that she wasn't to worry. A few hours later she received a War Office telegram advising her that her husband had been killed in action.[283]

In reporting the death, the Rossendale Free Press reporter wrote that "*General regret has been occasioned in Waterfoot by the announcement of the death in action of Lt Norman Whittaker of St*

---

[282] National Archives Ref WO95/2922
[283] Rossendale Free Press: 18 May 1918

James' Street. . .The late Lieutenant Whittaker was one of the best known young men in Waterfoot and was most highly esteemed."[284] He continued by commenting on Norman's pleasant disposition and listed the many posts he had held at St James's, noting that he had been one of the church's most valued members.[285]

Norman is buried in Plot VIII.F.17 at Lapugnoy Military Cemetery near Bethune in the Pas de Calais region of Northern France.

Norman Whittaker's Headstone
Lapugnoy Cemetery

---

[284] Rossendale Free Press: 18th May 1918
[285] Ibid

Private Sidney Worswick Ashworth
9th Battalion, Norfolk Regiment
Died 30th May 1918

Voormezeele Cemetery
Enclosure No. 3

Sidney Worswick Ashworth, born on 24th March 1899 at 157 New Line, Britannia, was the second youngest of six children born to Joseph and Elizabeth Ashworth. After first attending Britannia school, he was admitted to Newchurch Grammar School on 6th September 1911. The family were regular attenders at Beulah Methodist Church at New Line and Sidney went to the chapel Sunday School. As he grew older he was also associated with Irwell Terrace Sunday School. When he finished his education at Newchurch, he began working as an assistant in Dr Taylor's dental practice in Bacup.

Shortly before Sidney's 15th birthday, his father was killed in an accident at work. For many years, Joseph Ashworth had managed the Britannia Stone Quarry for Messrs Brooks and

Brooks. While working in the railway sidings near Britannia, he was knocked down by a stone-carrying wagon and badly injured. He was taken to Rochdale Infirmary but died from his injuries.[286]

Sidney's service record has not survived but some relevant information was found in both a local newspaper article written shortly after his death[287] and on the Forces War Records website.[288] Called up in April 1917, he was posted to the Norfolk Regiment and issued with service number 33150. Before the Military Service Act came into force in 1916, and assuming there were sufficient places available, a soldier could request to be assigned to a particular regiment. With the introduction of conscription, however, recruits no longer had a say in the matter and were assigned where the need was greatest. This may help to explain why Sidney Ashworth, a conscripted lad from a northern mill town, served as a Private in an East Anglian Regiment.

After an initial period of basic training, Sidney completed a signalling course at Grove Park in Kent and was posted to the Norfolk Regiment's 9th battalion in March 1918. At that date, this battalion was part of the 71st Brigade, 6th Division that was fighting in Flanders.

There was no gentle introduction to battalion life. When he arrived in Belgium, his unit had been at the front and under fire for some months, with only limited respite periods behind the lines. It is clear from the war diary that the troops were on constant alert for signs of an enemy advance that was expected at any time.[289] To ensure the battalion was ready in the event of an attack, listening patrols were sent out every night and observation posts were manned twenty-four hours

---

[286] Manchester Evening News: 2nd February 1914
[287] Bacup Times: 15th June 1918
[288] Forces-war-records.co.uk
[289] National Archives Ref WO 95/1623/2

a day. As soon as he arrived at the front, Sidney would have found himself under almost constant bombardment. During the brief periods out of the line, all four of the battalion's companies were engaged in constructing a new trench system, which was being built in an attempt to strengthen the line against the imminent attack.

The diary also notes that there was no time for any of the normal training sessions, kit inspections and periods of recreation that troops usually experienced when behind the lines. Even when they were withdrawn to reserve positions, working parties were still sent out regularly, under cover of darkness, to repair and strengthen trenches that were frequently damaged by constant German artillery attacks. A regular cycle for the troops was a few days in the front line trench, followed by time working further behind the line, before a return to the front to relieve their comrades in the line.

Despite these preparations, on 27th May the Germans mounted a swift and ferocious attack that succeeded in breaking through the allied front line. The following day, the 9th Norfolks took part in a counter-offensive, a successful assault that saw them take back territory that had been gained by the enemy. Preceded by a heavy artillery barrage on German lines, British troops began to move forward at 4am. The German reaction was swift and immediate and Sidney's battalion suffered under a heavy enemy artillery barrage as they made their advance.

The diary includes a casualty list for the month of May. This shows that a total of 16 other ranks were killed during that period, with 5 officers and another 485 other ranks wounded. Twenty-three were identified as gas victims. Private Ashworth is listed as having died on 30th May 1918. He was 19 years old and had been at the front for a mere nine weeks.

Since his mother had died in 1915, it was Sidney's brothers who received the letter from his commanding officer that explained the circumstances of his death. Captain Robert B Sanger had been in command of the battalion at the time, and wrote that Sidney and five of his comrades had been defending their trench "gallantly" against the enemy when all six had been killed by a shell. Captain Sanger added that Signalman Ashworth had always proved himself one of the best soldiers and was a man whom he feared they could ill spare.[290] He is remembered on the Bacup War Memorial.

As the war fronts ebbed and flowed, many bodies were left unburied or lay unrecognised in lost graves. By the time the armistice was signed, there were many hundreds of thousands of graves scattered about the various battlefields. Some were in isolated sites, hastily buried by their comrades, others buried in groups in small cemeteries or shell holes. To ensure that the graves of all those who had fallen received the respect and continual care they deserved, after the Armistice the Imperial War Graves Commission[291] took on the huge task of clearing the battlefields. Parties of soldiers were sent out to collect the remains of those who lay unburied and to exhume the bodies of those buried in solitary locations and from cemeteries with fewer than 40 graves. These men were then concentrated into larger pre-existing cemeteries or buried in newly created ones.

A Graves Registration Report Form is included with Sidney Ashworth's entry on the CWGC website. This shows that Sydney and five of his battalion comrades were exhumed in 1919, under the graves concentration arrangements. According to the report, four of the soldiers had also died on 30th May and the fifth was killed on the day before. The

---

[290] Bacup Times: 7 June 1918
[291] Established in May 1917 and now the Commonwealth War Graves Commission

remains of all six men were moved and reinterred at Voormezeele Enclosure Cemetery No3, a Commonwealth War Graves cemetery four miles south east of Ypres. All the men are buried in Plot XIV. Sidney and the others killed on 30th May are in a communal grave in Row E, Grave 5. The sixth soldier is buried in the same plot, Row C Grave 23.

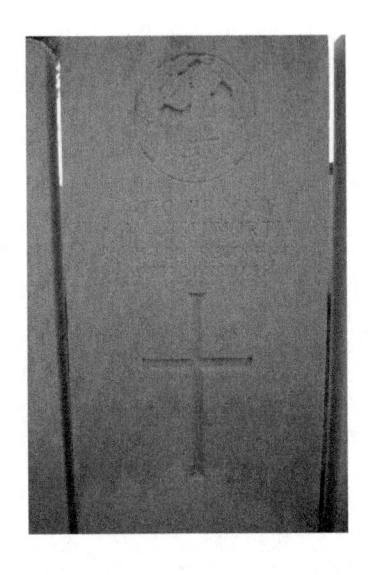

Headstone - Sidney Ashworth
Voormezeele Enclosure Cemetery No3

2nd Lieutenant Frank Warley Mitchell
2nd Battalion, Manchester Regiment
Died 7th June 1918

Remembered
Arras Memorial

Frank Warley Mitchell[292] was the son of elementary schoolmaster Frank Mitchell and his wife Mary. The couple lived at 2 Waterside Terrace in Bacup with their four sons, of whom Frank was the eldest. He was born on 6th June 1898 and attended Mount School in Bacup before he began his secondary education at Newchurch Grammar School on the 17th January 1911. When he left school in 1913, he began working as a clerk in the Bacup branch of the Manchester & County Bank.

On his eighteenth birthday in 1916, Frank became eligible for conscription although, under the terms of the Military Service Act of that year, he was not eligible for overseas service until he was nineteen years old. The age limit was

---

[292] Photograph: Reproduced by kind permission of NatWest Group © 2021

reduced to eighteen years and six months in April 1918, on condition that the recruit had been in training for six months.[293] The National Archives holds a file for Frank among the Officer Long Number Papers.[294] This shows that he signed up at Bacup on the day after his birthday in 1916, but was not mobilized until May 1917 when he was posted to the 64th Training Reserve Battalion as cadet 30818.

He appears to have acquitted himself well in the eyes of his superiors as, while undergoing training, he was put forward for a commission. His application was successful and he was admitted to the officer cadet battalion at Cambridge on 5th October 1917. He was gazetted on 27th February 1918 and posted as a 2nd Lieutenant to the 3rd battalion, Manchester Regiment. This was a home-based training unit and troops were accommodated with them while waiting to go overseas. Frank landed at Boulogne on 22nd April and made his way to the Infantry Base Depot at Étaples where he was assigned to the 2nd Battalion, Manchester Regiment.[295]

The 2nd battalion went to France in September 1914 as part of the British Expeditionary Force and took part in some of the major battles of the war: Mons, Le Cateau and Ypres. In December 1915 this experienced fighting unit was transferred to the 32nd Division to bolster the less experienced units fighting on the Western Front. In 1916 they saw action at the battles of Albert, Bazentin and the Ancre and pursued the Germans when they retreated back to their new stronghold at the Hindenburg Line. History would show that the 2nd Battalion lost more men during the Great War than any other Manchester battalion.

Fresh from training, Frank joined this highly experienced battalion on 26th April 1918. The unit had just returned from

---

[293] Despite these rules, some 250,000 under-age boys fought in WW1
[294] National Archives Ref WO 339/113338
[295] This battalion had been involved in the 1914 Christmas Truce.

front line duties where 14 of their rank had been killed and another 16 severely gassed. Shortly after his arrival, the battalion took up position at Blairville, near Arras. The war diary confirms that daily duties continued their regular pattern of working parties, raids, counter-raids and patrols.

Frank was hospitalised at Étaples in May after he had been found wandering around, barely conscious and suffering from trench fever.[296] He returned to his battalion on 2nd June. On the night of 6th/7th June, following an enemy incursion into the battalion's trench earlier in the day, Frank led a patrol out into No Man's Land. He never returned. The 2nd Manchester war diary describes the night's events.[297] *"Battalion in the line. The usual patrols were out, and listening posts established. A patrol under 2nd Lieutenant Mitchell went out to reconnoitre the enemy sap and trench from which point the enemy entered our posts the previous afternoon. This patrol encountered strong enemy opposition and the whole of them became casualties - 2nd Lieutenant Mitchell being afterwards reported as "missing". Casualties – 2 other ranks killed, 10 other ranks wounded and 5 other ranks wounded (gas)."* The next day's entry explained how Frank's comrades had made every effort to find him, but without success. *"A strong patrol under 2nd Lieutenant Bramley left our lines tonight to search for 2nd Lieutenant Mitchell, who failed to return from patrol the previous evening. The patrol in question met with strong enemy grenade opposition and bomb opposition, in consequence of which, the whole party became casualties - 2nd Lieutenant Bramley being killed. Casualties, 2 other ranks killed, 6 other ranks wounded and 4 other ranks wounded (gas)".*[298]

Frank Mitchell's officer file at the National Archives contains a large amount of correspondence relating to his disappearance and his father's desperate attempt to find out

---

[296] National Archives Ref WO 339/113338
[297] Punctuation and wording in the extracts has not been amended
[298] Excerpt with thanks to Liam Hart, former archivist Tameside MBC

what had happened to him.[299] One of the first documents is a copy of the telegram his parents received on 11th June advising them that their son was missing and that they should wait for more information. As the months passed and nothing more was heard, in growing frustration Mr Mitchell entered into correspondence with the War Office, his solicitor and his local MP. On 29th October, the War Office's Prisoner of War Bureau advised him that they had no news of Frank and suggested that he contact the Red Cross.

The next tranche of papers in the file begins in March 1919, with the War Office making enquiries abroad through the Netherlands Legation. On 15th March, a War Office memo stated that since nothing had come of these efforts, Lt Wilkinson's name was to be put forward for presumption of death in view of *"lapse of time."* Mr Wilkinson was advised of this decision, but no date of death was mentioned in the letter. On 31st March, the War Office wrote to the Army Records Office advising them that, in the absence of any further information and in view of the length of time that had elapsed since the date he was reported missing, 2nd Lt Mitchell had to be presumed dead for official purposes and that his death was said to have occurred on 7th June 1918. The memo is headed NOT TO BE COMMUNICATED OUTSIDE THE WAR OFFICE.[300]

Although a presumed date of death had been decided internally, Mr Mitchell was only advised that Frank was now presumed dead and that work would continue in an effort to find his grave. Not satisfied with this, Mr Mitchell continued searching for more information. He tracked down and interviewed one of the soldiers who had been in the patrol on the night it was attacked. The man was of the firm belief that

---

[299] National Archives Ref WO 339/113338
[300] National Archives Ref WO 339/113338

he had seen his Lieutenant running towards enemy lines in an attempt to take cover and that he didn't appear to have been injured. Since a thorough search had been made the next night, he had come to the conclusion that 2nd Lieutenant Mitchell had fallen into the hands of the enemy.[301]

Frank now firmly believed that his son could be alive and asked his local Rossendale MP, Robert Waddington, to intervene with the Secretary of State for War on his behalf. His conviction was strengthened in April 1920 when some of his son's effects were returned and appeared to his father to be clean and undamaged. He wrote to the War Office saying that he felt this indicated the items had been taken from Frank while he was alive, rather than removed from his body after death, and again pressed the authorities for more information. Their response was not encouraging. The items had been returned by the German government after the war but they had received no information as to the circumstances of their recovery. Furthermore, when the lists of missing soldiers had been sent to Germany after the war for clarification, the one that included the name of Lt Frank W Mitchell was returned with the German word TOT (dead) next to his name. With no other channels open to him, Mr Mitchell finally accepted that his son had died while on night patrol in 1918, on the day after his 20th birthday.

Frank's file also includes a letter written by his mother to the War Office. Dated 17th December 1919 it is the angry response of a grieving mother on receiving a scroll in her son's name. She was returning the scroll and explained, extremely forcibly, that she had "*absolutely no need of such a thing*" as she could look around her home and its surroundings at any time to see just what the family had suffered in losing Frank. She wrote at length of how proud

---

[301] National Archives Ref WO 339/113338

she was of her son's achievements, the sacrifices made to give him a good education which led to his obtaining a good job in a bank and his promises to look after his three brothers. In her eyes, the memorial scroll was an insult. It is retained in the file at the National Archives, together with Mrs Mitchell's letter.

Frank is remembered, with others of his regiment who have no known grave, on Bay 7 of the Arras Memorial. His name is also engraved on the Bacup War Memorial.[302]

Arras Memorial
Faubourg D'Amiens British Cemetery[303]

---

[302] This memorial is currently located within the ABDC Centre, Bacup
[303] Picture by courtesy of Alansart - Creative Commons License BY2.0

Sergeant James Pinnington
341st Road Construction Company, Royal Engineers
Died 30th July 1918

Aubigny Communal
Cemetery Extension

James Pinnington[304] was born in Whaley Bridge in Derbyshire on 3rd September 1882 and was the third child and only son of Richard and Margaret Pinnington. His father originally worked as a warehouse foreman in a calico print works, but by 1901 the census data shows that he was running his own Bookseller and Stationery business at 10 Bank Street, Rawtenstall. James started school at Clowbridge Baptist School before he went to Newchurch Grammar School, where he was admitted to the roll on 17th September 1894.

James left school in April 1896 and began working as an assistant to his father in the family business. By 1901, he was apprenticed to a local architect, Fred Hobson, but the change of career was temporary. Census data in 1911 indicates that

---

[304] Photograph: by kind permission of Hardman Lodge 1948, Rossendale Masonic Hall, Ashday Lea, Rawtenstall

James was a self-employed master letterpress printer. Having taken over the business when his father retired, he worked there until he joined the Army in April 1917.[305] He married Blanche Nightingale in 1908 and the couple had a daughter. He was a Freemason and a member of Rawtenstall Unitarian Church.

No service record survives, but a Medal Index Card is held at the National Archives.[306] This shows that James joined the Royal Engineers (RE) and was issued with service number 261242. He rose to the rank of Sergeant before his career took a new direction, following the intervention of a Royal Engineers' officer. James Johnson, a Captain in the 341st Road Construction Company (RCC), had been Rawtenstall's Borough Surveyor before the war. Being aware of James's prior surveying knowledge he arranged to secure his services as a non-commissioned officer in his own unit.

RCCs were one of many units that came under the auspices of the Royal Engineers. Where possible, the men in the units had experience of similar work in civilian life. They built new roads but more importantly, repaired existing networks that had been shattered by shellfire. This aided the flow of troops, artillery, ammunition and supplies and ensured that casualties could be transported back to the medical centres further behind the lines as quickly and smoothly as possible. The importance of roads made them prime targets for enemy artillery and the work of the RCC engineers was extremely dangerous and difficult. It had to be carried out in all weathers, twenty-four hours a day, to ensure that delays and disruption were kept to a minimum.

After a short period of training, James joined the 341st RCC as a Sergeant and was given the new serial number

---

[305] Rossendale Free Press: 10th August 1918
[306] National Archives Ref WO 372/16/14022

WR/26196.[307] Only a few months later, Mrs Pinnington received a telegram from the War Office advising her that, following an accident, her husband was dangerously ill at a casualty clearing station in France, but permission to visit him could not be granted.[308]

This news was quickly followed by a letter from Captain Johnson explaining the circumstances of the accident. James and a party of his men had been carrying out road repairs when James was knocked down by a lorry. On hearing of the accident, Captain Johnson had gone to the hospital immediately, but was informed on his arrival that James had died about half an hour after he had been admitted. The sister who had treated him said that he had been conscious when he arrived but was too badly injured to speak. Captain Johnson finished his letter by expressing how sorry he was and said that James had been a thoroughly reliable and loyal NCO.[309]

In a second letter received a few days later, Captain Johnson sent Mrs Pinnington details of her husband's funeral service. James had been carried to his grave by a number of his fellow NCOs and the service was attended by Captain Johnson and a group of the men who had worked under her husband. The service had been carried out "*in a most reverent manner*"[310] Some weeks later, the Rossendale Free Press carried a report of James's death and commented that "*his death was regretted by his comrades just as it was by his friends at home.*"[311]

---

[307] Introduced in March 1918, the WR prefix denoted RE troops involved in the construction of waterways, railways and roads.
[308] Rossendale Free Press: 10th August 1918
[309] Ibid
[310] Rossendale Free Press: 10 August 1918
[311] Ibid

In his letter, Captain Johnson informed Mrs Pinnington that her husband had died on 30th July 1918. The Register of Soldiers' Effects[312] shows that he died at the 42nd Casualty Clearing Station, which was located at Aubigny in the Pas de Calais. James is buried nearby; in Plot IV. F. 40 of Aubigny Communal Cemetery Extension.

At home in Rawtenstall, James is remembered on the town war memorial and on the WW1 memorial in front of the Unitarian Church on Bank Street. He was a Freemason and a member of Rawtenstall's Hardman Lodge 1948. The lodge erected a memorial to James and to a second Rawtenstall freemason who died in the Great War, Henry Carter. The carved wooden memorial, which includes pictures of the two men, is mounted on the wall of the Masonic Hall at Ashday Lea in Rawtenstall.

Grave of James Pinnington at Aubigny

---

[312] Available at Ancestry.co.uk

Chapter 12

The 1918 German Spring Offensive ended the four-year deadlock on the Western Front. Although they had been preparing their defences against an imminent assault, the strength and speed of the onslaught overwhelmed the Allies and they were pushed back over forty miles in a matter of days, the deepest advance into enemy-held territory by either side since the earliest days of the war. Despite their early success, the Germans were unable to inflict a decisive defeat on the Allies. When the attack ultimately failed, all hope of a German victory came to an end.

There was no one reason for the failure of the Spring Offensive. Strategically, the Germans had found it impossible to drive a wedge between the British and French armies and, although forced to retreat, the Allies were able to regroup and form new defensive lines. The Germans sustained a very high number of casualties and the strength of their army had diminished to such an extent that there were few reinforcements to bring forward as replacements. The Allies, on the other hand, had the advantage of being able to look to the Americans for reinforcements. Another major reason for failure was the speed of the German attack. So much ground was captured in such a short time that the troops moved too far forward of their railheads, with the result that they ran short of food, supplies and ammunition. Faced with these mounting difficulties, the attack stalled and was called off on 18th July. When planning the attack, the German High Command knew that it was their last chance to claim victory. They came very close to breaking through but, when they failed to do so, had no option but to go on the defensive.

The Allies were only too aware of the weakened German position and began to make preparations for a series of attacks that would ultimately lead them to victory. The first of these, the Battle of Amiens, began on 8th August and proved to be a stunning blow. Having coordinated an attack along the entire front, the Allies swiftly overcame German resistance, took 50,000 prisoners and captured 500 German guns. Over the next 100 days, the combined forces of the allied nations forced the German army back from most of the land it had occupied in France and Belgium.

2nd Lieutenant Harry Smith
9th Battalion, Manchester Regiment
Died 19th October 1918

Maurois Communal Cemetery
Le Cateau

Although the CWGC and Office of National Statistics census data use the legal forename Henry, his family always referred to him as Harry. This is the name engraved on the school Roll of Honour and printed in newspaper reports of his death. In view of this, the diminutive "Harry" has been used throughout this account.

Harry Smith[313] was born on 24th May 1890 and was the youngest of Edwin and Julia Smith's three children. The family lived at 68 Bank Street in Rawtenstall, from where Edwin ran his grocery business. After spending his formative years at Longholme Wesleyan School in the town, Harry was enrolled at Newchurch Grammar School on 30th April 1902. When he left, he began studying architecture, working as a junior architect at the offices of Mr Brocklehurst in

---

[313] Photograph: Rossendale Free Press 9th November 1918

Waterfoot. He later took up a post with Derbyshire Education Authority.[314]

Although no service record could be sourced at the National Archives, there is an Admission and Discharge record from 31st CCS in Harry's name.[315] This document shows that he enlisted shortly after war was declared and served as a 2nd Lieutenant in the 13th Manchester Regiment. This unit was raised in Ashton-under-Lyne in September 1914, as part of Kitchener's 3rd Army, and once at full strength, was sent to the south coast for training. First stationed at Seaford in East Sussex, they moved into billets in Eastbourne during the winter of 1914/15. With the return of warmer weather, the battalion returned to Seaford before they moved to Aldershot in May. They continued training until they were mobilized and sent to France in September 1915. They travelled south and joined the 22nd Division at their assembly point at Marseilles.[316]

The Division embarked for Salonika (now Thessaloniki) with orders to support the Serbian forces in their fight against the Bulgarian army. Under pressure to find replacement troops for other theatres of war, in particular France and Belgium, the War Office was reluctant to support this relatively quiet front in Greece with reinforcements. This eventually resulted in a gradual decline in troop numbers deployed to this somewhat forgotten front.

The 13th Battalion's deployment to Salonika lasted almost two years, yet they saw little action, taking part in one night attack and one four-day battle. They spent the majority of their time on routine patrols into the mountains, where they had to make their way over rough roads which, in many places, were little more than tracks. High rainfall in the area

---

[314] Rossendale Free Press: 9th November 1918
[315] National Archives Ref MH106/594
[316] wartimememories.co.uk

often turned these tracks to mud, creating great difficulties for food and ammunition supply routes. Bad as this was, the troops' worst enemy was malaria, which resulted in many casualties.

Harry's medical record at Kew relates to time he spent at the 31st Casualty Clearing Station at Sarigol while suffering from pyrexia (fever). Although there are no further details, there was a high incidence of both malaria and sand fly fever in the region. The day after he was admitted, he was transferred out of the area by ambulance train. The record does not indicate where he went, or for how long he was absent from his unit.

On 28th June 1918, Harry's battalion sailed from Salonika and disembarked in the south of France. Making their way north, they arrived at Abancourt near Amiens on 11th July, where they transferred to the 66th (2nd East Lancashire) Division who were already heavily involved in fighting on the Western Front. By August, the 13th Battalion were in position at Haudricourt, about 30 miles south west of Amiens, and commenced a training programme behind the lines. This was designed to prepare them for the conditions they would face fighting on the Western Front, conditions that were very different from those they had experienced in Salonika.

Around the time Harry arrived to fight in France, the ravages of war were having a dire effect on Field Marshall Haig's forces. The troops were weary from years of trench warfare and casualty rates had risen to such a high level that it was proving difficult to find enough men to bring battalions back up to full strength. Haig was particularly frustrated that thousands of capable men were being kept at home working in war-related industries rather than being sent out to fight at the front. Women had already shown that they could take up jobs in industry and Haig saw no reason why this work force could not be increased to release men for active service. He kept up pressure, advising the War Office that the only other alternative he had at his disposal was to reduce the total number of divisions across the front, effectively weakening it, and deploying the troops this would release among the remaining units.

The Cabinet Committee for Manpower disagreed with Haig and chose to find the additional men by reducing the number of battalions within each Division, rather than the number of Divisions. As a consequence, on 13th August 1918, the 13th Manchester Regiment was absorbed into the 9th Manchester battalion.

On 17th October, the allies began an attack along a ten-mile front south of Le Cateau with the aim of bringing the main German railway centre within range of the British artillery. The 9th Manchesters moved into the attack on 18th and early in the morning of 19th October they were subjected to heavy enemy machine gun fire and came under attack from German snipers. As dawn broke, it became clear that A Company was missing, with the exception of one man who had managed to make it back to the British lines. German artillery batteries continued to attack throughout the day and fired a number of gas shells onto the battalion's position. The decision was taken to send out a reconnaissance patrol and the war diary notes that during this operation, Lt H Smith and two other ranks were killed by a sniper.[317]

Harry Smith was 28 years old when he was killed. Having joined up early in the war, he died less than a month before the Armistice was signed. He is buried in plot 71.D at Maurois Communal Cemetery, Le Cateau and his name is included on the Rawtenstall War Memorial.

---

[317] National Archives Ref WO 95/3145/5

Maurois Communal Cemetery

Grave of Harry Smith

Chapter 13

As the opposing sides fought their way through what would prove to be the final months of the war, reports began to emerge of the increasing prevalence of a virulent strain of influenza. Although it is uncertain where the virus originated, it was first identified in a US Army camp in Kansas and spread rapidly among the troops and out into the general populace. To avoid lowering troop morale, wartime censors had suppressed news of just how virulent the virus was but as a neutral country, Spain was not bound by these restrictions and published the information. Although the virus did not originate in that country, the first information came from there and this is the most likely reason why the disease became known as Spanish Flu.

As American soldiers made their way across the Atlantic to join the war effort, they carried the virus with them, and in the confined quarters on board ship, the highly contagious disease was easily transmitted from soldier to soldier through coughing and sneezing. Once the troops landed in France, the virus spread to those whose resistance to disease had been severely weakened by many months spent living in the appalling conditions associated with trench warfare. Despite a rapid spread, mortality rates were relatively low.

Within a few months, the virus had travelled throughout Europe and beyond. Soldiers returning home on leave carried it across the English Channel, while Russian prisoners, released by Germany after the Treaty of Brest Litovsk, took it back to Russia. Ships' crews on supply routes were instrumental in transmitting it around the globe and by July 1918, now categorised as a global pandemic, the first cases began to appear in Australia. Shortly afterwards the virus appeared to recede.

A second, far more virulent wave struck towards the end of August. It proved to be far more deadly, with mortality rates highest among the 20 to 40 age group. Initially, patients contracted the influenza virus, which weakened their immune system to such an extent that they often developed severe bacterial pneumonia, a common secondary infection associated with virus. Pneumonia was the most common cause of death for those who were unable to fight off the initial influenza attack, and it could occur within a matter of hours.

On the Western Front, the pandemic spread among troops on both sides of the conflict, and hospitals and medical units were soon unable to cope with the enormous numbers of patients. Unable to find space to isolate those with the virus, it soon spread from the sick to the wounded and to both medical and nursing staff, many of whom died.

Two further waves followed before the pandemic came to an end in April 1920, but the last few months of 1918 saw the highest incidence of the disease. The speed at which the virus spread has been blamed on the repatriation of thousands of troops after the Armistice. Returning to homes and families around the globe, they unwittingly brought the virus with them and helped increase the transmission rate. Globally, by the time the pandemic came to an end it had been contracted by over 500,000 million people, around a third of the world's population in 1920. Of those infected, an estimated 50 million died, more than double the number of soldiers and civilians who died in WW1.

The Armistice that was signed on 11th November 1918 brought the war to an end, but it was many months before all the troops retuned home. In Britain, a demobilization system was put in place which gradually released soldiers back into civilian life, to prevent employment markets being flooded with returning troops looking for work. While waiting for release from military service, many soldiers found themselves posted to Germany as part of the occupying force agreed under the terms of the Armistice. A large number would never return to Britain. With the influenza pandemic at its height during the last few months of 1918, many of the troops contracted the virus and subsequently died. They now lie buried in one of four CWGC cemeteries in Germany. Three Newchurch Grammar School boys survived the war only to die during the pandemic. One is buried in France, one in Germany and one in Rossendale.

Sapper Edward Hall Holden
Depot Battalion, Royal Engineers
Died 7th November 1918

Rawtenstall Cemetery
Rossendale, Lancashire

Edward Holden, born in Rawtenstall on 22nd April 1897, was the son of William and Nora Holden. In the early years of the twentieth century, the family lived at 231 Bacup Road, Rawtenstall. By the date of the 1911 census, they had moved to 47 Bank Street, the main shopping street in the town, from where William ran his own grocery business. Edward went to Longholme School for his early education and then attended Newchurch Grammar School. The school's records show that he was admitted to the register on 2nd May 1910.

After he left school, he went to work as a clerk at the local cotton mill, Rawtenstall Manufacturing Company. He moved to the Newchurch Manufacturing Company and by the time war was declared he was working as a clerk for J K Haworth's mill at Reedsholme, on the outskirts of Rawtenstall.[318]

Although no service papers have been found, the CWGC database, the website Soldiers Died in the Great War[319] and the Rossendale Free Press archives provided a little information about Edward's Army service. He joined the Royal Engineers (RE) towards the end of 1916 as Sapper 278954 and served with L Company, Depot Battalion, based at Chatham in Kent. When reporting his death, the local newspaper informed its readers that *"On account of his previous clerical ability he was selected out of a large number to do clerical work in the RE's Record Office and has been so engaged practically since he entered the army."*[320]

Although Chatham is more usually associated with the historic naval dockyard, during WW1 it was the location of the Royal Engineer's training base, where new recruits underwent initial training. The base also trained members of the BEF who had returned to England to be assigned to the Engineers' specialist units and tunnelling companies. Edward worked with these specialist units.

After studying the few records that are still available, it is clear that Edward never served abroad during the war. The Depot Battalion to which he belonged was based at Chatham throughout the war and the website Soldiers Died in the Great War confirms that he was on permanent Home Service. Information on the Forces War Records website includes the detail that he died 'at home' on 7th November 1918, although this is slightly misleading. The description 'at home' is used to describe those soldiers who were posted to Home Service units, as opposed to those who served and

---

[318] Rossendale Free Press: 9th November 1918
[319] An 81 volume reference to British Army soldiers who died in WW1
[320] Rossendale Free Press: 9th November 1918

died abroad. It does not indicate that a man died at his home address. This is confirmed by an entry in the Record of Soldiers' Effects which shows that Edward died at Fort Pitt Military Hospital, Chatham.[321]

According to newspaper reports, Edward's parents had received a telegram on Saturday 2nd November 1918 to say that their son was ill and had been admitted to hospital in Chatham. They travelled down to Kent to be with him and, on arrival, found him to be suffering from pneumonia, as a consequence of having contracted influenza. *"From the time of their arrival, either the father or mother were (sic) in constant attendance but unfortunately the young man passed away at 2am last Thursday."*[322] Edward was 21 years old when he died and had been in the army for two years.

His body was brought back to Rawtenstall, where it was laid to rest in a family grave in Rawtenstall Cemetery. As he was buried with members of his family, his grave is not marked by the familiar CWGC headstone associated with military burials but with a family headstone. His name is inscribed with other members of his family, including two of his siblings who had died in infancy. His parents' names were later added, his father's in 1943 and his mother's in 1961.

Edward's name is inscribed on the memorial to former Sunday school scholars that stands in the grounds of Longholme Methodist Church, the church where he was considered to have been *"a most promising young man."*[323] Other than the memorial at BRGS, this is the only memorial to Edward, as his name has not been included on the town's municipal war memorial. This may have been at his family's request.

---

[321] Register available to view at Ancestry.
[322] Rossendale Free Press: 9th November 1918
[323] Ibid

War memorials were constructed in towns and villages throughout the country. They gave those who had lost loved ones somewhere to go to mourn and remember them. Most were constructed after the war, but the Rawtenstall War Memorial, coincidently located in the cemetery in which Edward is buried, was erected in 1915 and is recognised by the Imperial War Museum as the first community WW1 memorial to have been erected in England. It is a Grade III listed historic monument.[324]

Municipal War Memorial in Rawtenstall Cemetery

---

[324] Historic England gave it a listing in 1999. The monument was restored in time for the centenary commemorations.

Private Richard Crawshaw Hardman
Royal Army Service Corps
Died 19th November 1918

Busigny Communal Cemetery Extension
Le Cateau, France

Richard Hardman was born in Haslingden on 29th January 1894. He was the son of cotton manufacturer George Walter Hardman and his wife Eleanor. The couple had four other children, one of whom died in infancy. They first lived at Whitecroft Mount in Haslingden but later moved to "Danesmoor", a large detached villa on Helmshore Road, Haslingden. Records in the BRGS archives indicate that he attended Church School in Haslingden before he enrolled at NGS on 14th January 1904.[325] When he left school, he was

---

[325] There is nothing to identify to which church the school belonged

employed as a book-keeper in a local cotton mill, although there is nothing in the census to confirm whether this was his father's mill.

According to his service papers,[326] Richard signed his Short Service Attestation on 19th March 1915, when he was 21 years old. His civilian occupation is given as a motor driver, although there is nothing in any of the records to indicate when he gave up book keeping to take up this new employment. His new career may well have been taken into consideration when he joined the army, as he was assigned to the Mechanical Transport Depot of the Army Service Corps. He was issued with the service number M2/053949 and attached to 142nd (Durham) Heavy Battery, Royal Garrison Artillery (RGA)

The RGA's heavy batteries were equipped with the army's largest artillery pieces and the 142nd Heavy Battery fired 6 x 6 inch howitzers. Positioned back from the front, these heavy guns fired high explosive shells which were used to destroy or neutralise enemy artillery positions and weaponry. They also targeted the enemy's transport, communication systems, ammunition dumps and strongholds.

Richard was based in England until 21st March 1916, when the battery embarked for France and from May 1916 until January 1918, he worked with various Mechanised Transport Companies (MTCs).[327] During WW1, the British Army was the most advanced in the use of motor transport. Men like Richard drove the 3 ton, four-wheel drive lorries that hauled the heavy artillery to new positions. MTC drivers also resupplied the guns with ammunition.

Richard's final posting was to the 18th Divisional MTC. He joined them in January 1918 when they were repositioning the guns of the 142nd Heavy Battery to their new firing

---

[326] Accessed through Ancestry
[327] The 272nd, 604th and 611th MTC

positions around Arras and Amiens. By the date of the Armistice he was at Reget-de Beaulieu, some 20 miles south east of Cambrai.[328]

Sadly, having survived the war, Richard was never to return home to Lancashire. According to a short report written by an RAMC Captain and contained within Richard's service papers, he was admitted to the 37th Casualty Clearing Station at Busigny five days after the Armistice suffering from influenza. A second wave of the virus had emerged in the autumn of 1918 and those aged 20 to 40 were proving to be more susceptible to this deadly mutation. Shortly after he was admitted, Richard developed broncho-pneumonia and his condition deteriorated rapidly over the next three days. He died on 19th November at the age of 24 and was buried at Busigny Communal Cemetery Extension in grave VIII.C.26.

The village of Busigny is about 10 kilometres south east of Le Cateau and was captured by the Americans during the Battle of Cambrai in October 1918. Shortly after the Germans retreated from the town, it became the site of successive allied Casualty Clearing Stations and the 37th CCS was there from early November 1918 until January 1919. The majority of burials in Busigny cemetery are from these CCSs.

After Richard's death, a local newspaper reported that a Major A D Spooner had written to Mrs Hardman: "*Your son had served under me for about a year, certainly the hardest and most strenuous year of the war to us. His work was always most conscientiously and cheerfully carried out, the more often than not under the most trying and dangerous conditions. His duties brought him into touch with almost every member of the unit, and there are few men who have been more universally respected and loved than your boy was. As his commanding officer I feel probably more even than the others your deep sense of loss. His steadiness of character and excellent example*

---

[328] Today the town is known as Rejet-de-Beaulieu

made him more to the unit than words can express, and in losing him we lose a good friend and a very brave soldier. I am enclosing a little drawing of the oak cross we placed over his grave, which is in Busigny military cemetery, not far from Le Cateau. The men are making a memorial tablet which will be sent to you in due course, and we feel you may value this more than anything of a more temporary nature." [329]

A comrade of Richard's also wrote to Mrs Hardman and mentioned her son's cheery smile and ever ready willingness to help. He had never been seen to hesitate or to fail in carrying out his duty. *"He lived as you would have him live, and died as he lived - a very true and gallant gentleman."* [330]

Richard is remembered on the Haslingden Roll of Honour in Haslingden Public Library. He was one of many millions of soldiers and civilians who died in the 'Spanish Flu' pandemic.

Busigny Communal Cemetery Extension

---

[329] Haslingden Guardian: 3rd December 1918
[330] Ibid

Lance Corporal Reginald Alfred Stock
302 Road Construction Company, Royal Engineers
Died 20th February 1919

South Cemetery
Cologne, Germany

Reginald Alfred Stock was born in Honiton, Devon on 24th October 1889. He was the second of three children born to the Rev Alfred Stock and his wife Elizabeth. Alfred was a Baptist minister and after working in his home county for a number of years, he moved to the North West in 1897 to take up the vacant position at Waterbarn Baptist Church, a flourishing congregation in the village of Stacksteads.[331] The family lived at Underwood House in Bacup and Reginald

---

Headstone photograph by The War Graves Photographic Project
[331] bacuptimes.co.uk/index_htm_files/Waterbarn-Baptist.pdf

first attended the Board School in the town (originally the church day school). He was enrolled at Newchurch Grammar School on 18th April 1901 and later moved to Rochdale Technical School as a pupil teacher. Once qualified, he taught at Western Council School in Stacksteads.

In 1907 Rev Stock became pastor of Sheffield Road Baptist Church in Barnsley.[332] Reginald moved to Yorkshire with his parents, and with the move to Yorkshire came a change of career. According to De Ruvigny's Roll of Honour,[333] he trained as a mining surveyor and when he qualified he worked at the Wharncliffe Silkstone Colliery near Barnsley. He was also a member of the Midland Institute of Mining Engineers.[334]

Only some of Reginald's service papers survived the 1940 London Blitz and these are badly scorched, making them difficult to read. His attestation document shows that he enlisted at Barnsley on 10th December 1915 and was sent to the Reserve to await mobilization. The date suggests that Reginald was another from NGS who enlisted under Lord Derby's Group Scheme, introduced in an attempt to avoid the introduction of conscription.

By 1915, casualty rates were continuing to rise, particularly on the Western Front. Although there was an urgent need to bring units back to fighting strength, the number of recruits had fallen away after an initial rush to enlist in the early months of the war. The Derby Scheme, as it became known, was introduced in an attempt to increase the number of new volunteers. Under the scheme, men could enlist but then continue in their civilian occupations until such time as the Army mobilized, equipped and trained

---

[332] genuki.org.uk/BarnsleySheffieldRoadBaptistChurch
[333] Accessed at Find My Past
[334] Information provided by Chris Jones - Friends of Hemingfield Colliery

them and sent them off to fight, a process that could take many months. The scheme failed to entice sufficient numbers to come forward, and this ultimately led to the introduction of conscription in 1916.

Almost a year passed before Reginald was called to attend his medical board in Pontefract, a couple of months after he celebrated his twenty-seventh birthday. Although he was passed fit, his medical record was stamped with the addendum that, due to his very poor eyesight, he was not to be considered for General or Garrison Service abroad, but could serve as a non-combatant.[335]

On 8th December he joined the 302nd Road Construction Company (RCC) of the Royal Engineers as a Pioneer and was issued with the service number WR/20379.[336] He embarked for France on 15th January 1917. He sat and passed his RE skills test and was reclassified as a Sapper on 13th June 1917. Eighteen months later, on 22nd December 1918, he was promoted to the rank of Lance Corporal.

Reginald's service record includes his casualty form, which shows that he was admitted to hospital on two separate occasions, for fifteen days in April 1917 and for about a month in May 1918, but there is nothing to say where the hospitals were located or why he was admitted.

In accordance with the terms of the Armistice,[337] allied military personnel began to move into Germany on 1st December 1918 and took up positions along the Rhine. This was done to protect France from any possibility of a renewed German attack. The first indication that Reginald was posted to Germany with the Army of Occupation is a casualty form among his service papers noting that had died at 29th CCS on

---

[335] He was classified as 6/36; at a distance of 6ft he could read a line of letters normal sighted people could read at 36ft
[336] WR signified waterways and railways section
[337] The Long Long Trail - longlongtrail.co.uk/battles

20th February 1919, just a few weeks before his thirtieth birthday.

A number of Casualty Clearing Stations had followed the allies into Germany and set up base hospitals to support the needs of the occupying troops. In her war diary, the Matron-in Chief of Nursing Services, Maud McCarthy, states the precise location of 29 CCS at the date of Reginald's death.[338] In early March, she had toured a number of CCSs in Germany, first at Cologne and then at Bonn. On 2nd March 1919, she wrote that, whilst at Bonn, she had visited the recently opened 29 CCS. Reginald's entry in De Ruvigny's Roll of Honour confirms that he died at Bonn and was buried in Popplesdorfer Cemetery in the city.[339]

The local press published an obituary for Reginald and reported that his widowed mother had received written notification that her son had been admitted to hospital on 19th February and had died the following day from heart failure, as a result of influenza, complicated by pneumonia. The newspaper reported that Reginald's death had come as a great shock to his family as they had been expecting him home on leave. The obituary continued *"He was of such a cheery disposition that all who knew him loved him and his many friends will be distressed to hear of his early death"*.[340] His commanding officer also spoke highly of "Reggie" and said that he *"did exceptionally fine work whilst with the Company. He was always most cheery and bright and nothing was too much for him to do. He was one of whom it could truly be said that the world at large, and this company in particular, will be the poorer for his loss"*.[341]

In total, there were 180 burial grounds across Germany for Commonwealth soldiers who had died during the war, the

---

[338] scarletfinders.co.uk
[339] De Ruvigney's Roll of Honour accessed at Ancestry
[340] Bacup Times: 8th March 1919
[341] Ibid

majority of whom had been prisoners of war. In addition, there were others like Reginald, who had died from illness or injury while serving in Germany after the Armistice. In 1922, it was decided to concentrate all the graves into four main cemeteries at Kassel, Berlin, Hamburg and Cologne. Reginald was one of 133 servicemen whose remains were removed from Poppelsdorfer Cemetery and reburied at Cologne Southern Cemetery. He was reinterred on 6th December, 1923 in plot XII.C.10. Today, the cemetery lies within the grounds of Sudfriedhof civilian cemetery in Cologne. Reginald is remembered on the Roll of Honour at Sheffield Road Baptist Chapel in Barnsley.

A few documents in Reginald's file record his mother's struggle to have her son's personal effects returned to her; in particular his watch and fountain pen, presents from his father, who had since died. After some months, Mrs Stock was advised that, since both 302nd RCC and 29th CCS had now been disbanded, they regretted that there was nothing more that could be done to trace the missing items.

Cologne Southern Cemetery[342]

---

[342] Picture courtesy of Rutland Remembers – www.rutlandremembers.org

Chapter 14

Many men from towns and villages around Rossendale went to war. Over 675 didn't return and are remembered on war memorials around the valley. The largest and most imposing of these are the municipal memorials in Rawtenstall, Bacup, Haslingden and Helmshore. Smaller memorials, books of remembrance and rolls of honour were created in memory of former work colleagues, members of local clubs, societies, churches and schools.

Although the histories of thirty-seven young men have been recounted in this volume, other former NGS pupils played their part but, having survived the conflict, their names are not inscribed on any of the memorials. Those former pupils who returned home have passed into history, and are now anonymous to all but their families.

The Newchurch Grammar School Roll of Honour was unveiled by the former headmaster, Mr T E Jackson, on Saturday 15th October 1921 and was engraved with thirty-five names. At some later date an additional two names were added.

Appendix

In recent years, lower school history students at BRGS have made an annual 3-day visit to the battlefields of France and Belgium. Accompanied by members of staff and led by professional battlefield guides, they tour some of the major battlegrounds of the Somme and Flanders. Pupils lay a number of wreaths: at the Menin Gate, at the Accrington Pals' Memorial at Sheffield Park and at Tyne Cot Cemetery near Ypres. A ceremony at Tyne Cot is the last event of the tour and is particularly poignant as the names of two of the old boys, Percy Horsfield and Arthur Taylor, are engraved on the memorial walls that surround the cemetery.

During the 2019 visit, pupils and staff were honoured with a private service at St George's Memorial Church in Ypres during which a plaque was unveiled in memory of the thirty seven former pupils. The church was built as a memorial to all British and Commonwealth soldiers who died in the two world wars and contains over four hundred memorials to regiments, associations, and individuals.

St George's Memorial Church, Ypres

Bibliography & Sources

Unit Histories

History of the East Lancashire Regiment in the Great War 1914-1918 (Original publisher Littlebury Bros Ltd, 1936. Republished by The Duke of Lancaster's Regiment)

Coop, Rev J.O. *The Story of the 55th (West Lancashire Division)* (Liverpool: Daily Post Printers 1919, republished Naval & Military Press)

Drum, N. & Dowson, R. *'God's Own' 1st Salford Pals 1914-1916. An account of the 15th (Service) Battalion Lancashire Fusiliers.* (Neil Richardson, 2003)

Gibbon, F.P. *The 42nd (East Lancashire) Division 1914-1918* (London: Country Life Ltd 1920. Reprinted by Naval & Military Press, 2003)

Hurst, S. *The Public Schools Battalion in the Great War. 'Goodbye Piccadilly'* (Pen & Sword Ltd, 2007)

Mace, M. & Grehan, J. *Slaughter on the Somme 1 July 1916. The Complete War Diaries of the British Army's Worst Day.* (Pen & Sword Military, 2013)

Morris, J. *The Church Lads' Brigade in the Great War. The 6th (Service) Battalion The King's Royal Rifle Corps* (Pen & Sword Military, 2015)

Stedman, M. *Salford Pals. 15th, 16th, 19th & 20th Battalions Lancashire Fusiliers. A History of the Salford Brigade.* (Pen & Sword, 2016)

Stedman, M. *Manchester Pals 16th, 17th, 18th, 19th, 20th, 21st, 22nd & 23rd Battalions of the Manchester Regiment. A History of the Two Manchester Brigades* (Pen & Sword, 2016)

Falls, Capt C. *The Official History: Military Operations in France and Belgium 1917 Volume I* (London: Macmillan & Co Ltd 1940)

General Books

Duncan, G.S. *Douglas Haig As I Knew Him* (First Published by Allan & Unwin, 1966. Edition by Pen & Sword, 2015)

Groom, W. *A Storm in Flanders. Triumph and Tragedy on the Western Front* (London: Cassell Military Paperbacks, 2004)

Harrison, M. *High Wood* (Pen & Sword Military, 2017)

Hastings, M. *Catastrophe. Europe Goes To War* (London: William Collins, 2013)

Kendall, P. *Somme 1916. Success and Failure on the First Day of the Battle of the Somme* (Frontline Books, 2015)

Liddle, P. *The 1916 Battle of the Somme Reconsidered* (Pen & Sword, 2016)

Liddle, P. (editor) *Britain Goes to War. How the First World War Shaped the Nation* (Pen & Sword Ltd, 2015)

Living, E.G.G & Gibbs, Sir P. *Walking Into Hell. The Somme through British and German Eyes* (Pen & Sword Military, 2014)

Lloyd, N. *Passchendaele A New History* Viking, 2017)

Longworth, P. *The Unending Vigil. The History of the Commonwealth War Graves* Commission (Pen & Sword Military, 2010)

Lynch, E.P.F. edited by Davies, W. *Somme Mud. The Experiences of an Infantryman in France 1914 – 1916* (Doubleday, 2008)

Macdonald, L. *Somme* (London: Papermac, 1987)

Macdonald, L. *They Called it Passchendaele. The Story of the Third Battle of Ypres and of the men who fought in it.* (London: Penguin, 1993)

Macdonald, L. *To the Last Man Spring 1918* (Viking, 1998)

Mallinson, A. *Fight to the Finish. The First World War – Month by Month* (London: Bantam Press, 2018)

Middlebrook, M. *1st July 1916. The First Day on the Somme* (London: Penguin History, 2006)

Moore, W. *The Thin Yellow Line* (Ware, Herts: Wordsworth Military Library,1999)

Mure, A.H. and Van Emden, R. *This Bloody Place. The Incomparables at Gallipoli* (originally published 1919. Pen & Sword 2015)

Neillands, R. *The Great War Generals on the Western Front 1914-18* (London: Robison Publishing, 1998)

Nicholls, J. *Cheerful Sacrifice. The Battle of Arras 1917* (Pen & Sword, 2013)

Norman, T. *The Hell They Called High Wood* (Pen & Sword Military, 2014)

Rawson, A. *Somme Offensive 1918.* (Pen & Sword, 2018)

Rawson, A: *The Final Advance. September to November 1918* (Pen & Sword, 2018)

Rogerson, S. with introduction by Brown, M. *Twelve Days on the Somme. A Memoir of the Trenches 1916* (Greenhill Books, 2006 edition)

Scotland, T. and Heys, S. *Understanding the Somme 1916. An Illuminating Battlefield Guide.* (Helion & Co, 2014)

Simkins, P. *Kitchener's Army. The Raising of the New Armies 1914 – 1916* (Manchester University Press in Association with the Imperial War Museum, 2014)

Van Emden, R. *Missing. The Need for Closure after the Great War* (Pen & Sword, 2019)

Wilkinson, R. *Pals on the Somme 1916* (Pen & Sword, 2014)

Westlake, R. *Tracing British Battalions on the Somme* (Pen & Sword Military, 2009)

War Diaries – National Archives References

No10 Casualty Clearing Station WO 95/342/6
No17 Casualty Clearing Station WO 95/343/6
No37 Casualty Clearing Station WO 95/499/6
No48 Casualty Clearing Station WO 95/500/5
11th Battalion Cheshire Regiment WO 95/2250/1
1/5th Battalion, East Lancashire Regiment WO 95/2657/1
2nd Battalion, East Lancashire Regiment WO 95/1720/2
2/4th Battalion, East Lancashire Regiment WO 95/3141/3
2/5th Battalion, East Lancashire Regiment WO95/3141/5
8th Battalion, East Lancashire Regiment WO 95/2537/4
140th Field Ambulance WO 95/2630/1
12th Battalion, King's Liverpool Regiment WO 95/2126/2
King's Own Royal Lancaster Regiment WO 95/2922
16th Battalion, King's Royal Rifle Corps WO 95/2430/3
2nd Battalion, Lancashire Fusiliers WO 95/1507/1 and WO 95/1507/2
2/5th Battalion, Lancashire Fusiliers WO 95/2923/2
15th Battalion, Lancashire Fusiliers WO 95/22397/3
2/5th Battalion, Manchester Regiment WO 95/3144/6
9th Battalion, Manchester Regiment WO 95/3145/5
21st Battalion, Manchester Regiment WO 95/1668/3
9th Battalion, Norfolk Regiment WO 95/1623/2
276th Brigade, Royal Field Artillery WO 95/2914/4
177th Siege Battery, Royal Garrison Artillery WO 95/296/3
92nd Brigade Machine Gun Company WO 95/2358/2
2nd Battalion, Royal Marine Light Infantry WO 95/3110/2
431st Field Company, Royal Engineers WO 95/3129/4
33rd Light Railway Company, Royal Engineers WO 95/4056/3
2nd Royal Marine Battalion WO 95/3110/2
1st Battalion, South Wales Borderers WO 95/1280/3
10th Battalion, West Yorkshire Regiment WO 95/2004/1

Newspapers & Articles

Clark, P.L. Papers relating to BRGS Memorial Roll Research, 2003 now held in the BRGS Archives

Friends of BRGS Newsletter No 16, Winter 2008

Bacup Times

Bacup Chronicle

Blackpool Herald

Blackpool Times

Haslingden Guardian

Lancashire Evening Post

Lancashire Daily Post

Liverpool Post & Daily Mercury

London Gazette

Manchester Evening News

Rossendale Free Press

Yorkshire Post

Websites

Ancestry UK www.ancestry.co.uk
British Library https://www.bl.uk
Bacup Home Front www.bacuptimes.co.uk
Bacup & Rawtenstall Grammar School www.brgs.org.uk
Bolton Church Institute School War Memorial www.bolton-church-institure.org.uk
Bury Archives Online   www.buryarchivesonline.co.uk
Commonwealth War Graves Commission www.cwgc.org.uk
Creative Commons https://creativecomons.org
Find My Past www.findmypast.co.uk
Friends of Hemmingfield Colliery www.hemmingfielddcolliery.rg
Forces War Records www.forces-war-records.co.uk
Free BMD Online www.bmd.org.uk
Genealogy Forum www.genealogy.com
Great War Forum www.greatwarforum.co.uk
Haslingden War Heroes hrrps://haslingdenwarheroes.blogspot.com
History Hit www.historyhit.com by Snow, D
Imperial War Museum www.iwm.org.uk

Internet Archive https://archive.org
Lancashire Free BMD   www.lancashirebmd.org.uk
Lancashire Parish Clerk Online   www.lan-opc.org.uk
Lancashire Post www.lep.co.uk
Lijssenthoek Military Cemetery www.lijssenthoek.be
Manchester Grammar School and the First World War - https://sites.google.com
National Museum Royal Navy www.nnrn.org
Natwest Group Remembers www.natwestgroupremembers.com
Naval History.Net www.naval-history.net
Rawtenstall War Memorial www.rawtenstallwarmemorial.org
Rossendale Family History Society www.rossendalefhhs.org.uk
Royal Marines History www.royalmarineshistory.com
Rutland Remembers www.rutlandremembers.org
St George's Church Ypres www.stgeorgesmemorialchurchypres.com
Scarlet Finders: British Military Nurses www.scarletfinders.co.uk
Scotland's People www.scotlandspeople.gov.uk
Soldiers of Shropshire Museum www.shropshireregimentalmuseum.co.uk
Tameside Local Studies & Archives www.tameside.gov.uk
The Dreadnought Project www.dreadnoughtproject.org
The National Archives www.nationalarchives.gov.uk
The Long Long Trail www.longlongtrail.co.uk   Baker, C.
The National Museum Royal www.nmrn.org
The University of Manchester www.manchester.ac.uk
The War Graves Photographic Project www.twgpp.org
UK & Ireland Genealogy www.genuki.org
US Army www.army.mil - Garamone, J. "Building the American Military"
Wartime Memories Project www.wartimememoriesproject.com
World War One Battlefields ww1battlefileds.co.uk
World War One War Graves www.ww1wargraves.co.uk

Index

Aisne, 150
Andrew, Ronald 5, 75
Armistice, 177, 195, 197, 205, 209, 210
Army Service Corps, 130, 132, 203, 204 (ASC), 130
Arras, 44, 57, 62, 65, 66, 67, 68, 71, 72, 73, 74, 75, 76, 102, 106, 111, 112, 113, 125, 126, 140, 155, 156, 179, 181, 184, 204, 215
Ashworth, Sidney 170
Aspden, Albert 36, 40
Battle of Arras, 66, 75
Aubers Ridge, 11, 12
Aubigny Communal Cemetery Extension, 185, 188
Bacup & Rawtenstall Grammar School (BRGS), 3, 5, 1, 9, 33, 68, 84, 86, 93, 95, 108, 146, 165, 201, 203, 213, 21
Bacup and Rawtenstall Secondary School, 10
Bacup Times, 5, 33, 55, 63, 90, 91, 108, 123, 125, 164, 166, 167, 175, 177, 210, 217
Bacup War Memorial, 67, 167, 178, 184
Bandaghem, 85, 153, 157, 158
Battle of Amiens, 190
Battle of Broodseinde, 107, 108
Battle of Cambrai, 205
Battle of Gavrell, 71
Battle of Neuve Chapelle, 59
Battle of the Ancre, 56
Battle of the Lys, 141, 157

Battle of the Scarpe, 74
Newchurch Grammar School, 3, 5, 1, 14, 26, 33, 39, 42, 48, 53, 57, 58, 62, 68, 73, 79, 84, 89, 95, 100, 110, 116, 124, 129, 148, 154, 155, 159, 168, 174, 179, 185, 192, 199, 207, 212
Bethune, 13, 15, 16, 118, 136, 142, 168, 171, 173
Booth, Alan 24, 26, 28
BRGS Roll of Honour, 12, 1, 5, 9, 10, 67, 84, 86, 92, 93, 95, 133, 146, 191, 206, 208, 210, 211, 212
British Expeditionary Force (BEF) 3, 5, 7, 26, 80, 132, 160, 180, 200
Busigny Communal Cemetery, 203, 205, 206
Cape Helles, 19, 130
Casualty Clearing Stations(CCS) 16, 27, 85, 121, 137, 156, 157, 162, 188, 192, 193, 205, 209, 210, 211, 216
Caterpillar Valley Cemetery, 38, 41
Chatham Naval Memorial, 55
Cheshire Regiment, 79, 80, 216
Clark, Philip 5, 9, 33, 84, 93, 95, 217
Collinge, James 155
Commonwealth War Graves Commission, (CWGC) 14, 16, 19, 20, 25, 29, 58, 63, 68, 84, 99, 101, 103, 104, 108, 115, 117, 122, 133, 167, 169, 177, 191, 198, 200, 201, 215, 217

Crowther, Wilfred 56, 59, 61
Dardanelles, 17, 19, 130, 131
De Ruvigny's Roll, 10, 208, 210
Delville Wood, 106
Derby Scheme, 4, 106, 129, 208
Dozinghem, 83, 85, 86
East Lancashire Regiment, 58, 59, 61, 62, 63, 64, 65, 66, 73, 74, 100, 101, 102, 105, 116, 117, 119, 148, 169, 170, 214, 216
East Lancs, 59, 63, 64, 65, 66, 102, 103, 117, 118, 119, 120, 135, 136, 148, 150, 151
Eastern Cemetery Boulogne, 167
Étaples, 125, 155, 156, 180, 181
Fielding Tom, 46, 49, 51
Flanders, 6, 11, 17, 20, 22, 23, 24, 26, 77, 81, 82, 85, 96, 97, 98, 99, 108, 109, 118, 120, 141, 144, 150, 175, 213, 214
France, 3, 5, 7, 9, 10, 13, 15, 17, 20, 22, 26, 28, 30, 33, 34, 38, 42, 44, 59, 62, 63, 64, 65, 68, 69, 70, 73, 75, 76, 77, 84, 85, 100, 111, 117, 118, 123, 124, 130, 131, 135, 139, 143, 144, 145, 148, 150, 155, 160, 164, 165, 167, 168, 170, 173, 179, 180, 185, 187, 190, 191, 192, 193, 196, 203, 204, 209, 213, 214, 215
Gallipoli, 17, 64, 69, 117, 130, 131, 215
German Spring Offensive, 36, 41, 98, 140,141, 145, 151,189
Ginchy, 45, 46, 85
Guillemont, 85, 106
Haig, Earl 11, 56, 76, 77, 96, 98, 121, 193, 194, 214
Haldane Army Reforms, 85, 144
Hardman, Richard 199

Haringhe Military Cemetery, 157
Harvey, Joseph 79
Haslingden Guardian, 5, 124, 126, 128, 129, 131, 206, 217
Haslingden Municipal War Memorial, 76
Heys, Michael 149, 154,
Hitchen, Frank 50
Hawthorn Ridge, 31
High Wood, 39, 40, 41, 106, 124, 214, 215
Hindenburg Line, 106, 180
Holden, Edward 195
Holt, Albert 144
Horrocks, Frank 85,
Horsfield, Percy 101,
Howorth, Fred 65
Hunter-Weston, 31
Hutchinson, James 9, 7, 12
influenza, 196, 197, 198, 201, 205, 210
Jackson, Edward 8
Jackson, Ernest 32
Battle of Jutland, 47, 87
Kemmel, 157, 162
Kemmelberg, 157, 162
King's Liverpool Regiment, 144, 216
King's Own Royal Lancaster Regiment, (KORLR)169, 170
King's Royal Rifle Corps, 38, 39, 214, 216
King's Shropshire Light Infantry, 80
King's Royal Rifle Brigade
King's Royal Rifles, 39
King's Royal Rifle Corps Church Lads' Brigade, 39, 214
Kitchener, Lord 3, 5, 7, 14, 24, 44, 64, 124, 192, 216

La Bassée canal,, 172
Lancashire & Yorkshire Bank, 19, 21, 26, 29, 168
Lancashire & Yorkshire Railway Company, 159
Lancashire Daily Post, 169, 217
Lancashire Fusiliers, 6, 18, 19, 20, 33, 34, 42, 43, 44, 45, 74, 75, 214, 216
Lapugnoy Military Cemetery, 168, 173
Le Cateau, 180, 191, 194, 195, 203, 205, 206
Le Touret Memorial, 12
Light Railway Companies, 159, 160, 161, 162, 216
Lijssenthoek Military Cemetery, 25, 28, 29, 134, 138, 218
Liverpool Post & Daily Mercury, 19, 21, 217
London Regiment, 74
Artists Rifles, 74
Machine Gun Corps, 123, 125
Manchester & County Bank, 79, 179
NatWest Group, 5, 79, 80, 179
Manchester Evening News, 15, 26, 35, 36, 43, 175, 217
Manchester Regiment, 6, 19, 59, 105, 106, 143, 144, 145, 179, 180, 191, 192, 194, 214, 216
Marne, 7, 22
Maurois Communal Cemetery, 191, 195
Mechanical Transport Company, 204
Mendinghem, 85
Menin Gate, 79, 82, 118, 120, 137, 213
Messines, 77, 78, 81, 82, 96

Military Service Act, 101, 175, 179
Mitchell, Frank 175
National Archives, 6, 12, 16, 19, 20, 21, 27, 34, 40, 43, 44, 49, 59, 60, 61, 63, 70, 74, 75, 76, 80, 84, 86, 94, 101, 103, 111, 113, 124, 125, 126, 127, 131, 132, 144, 146, 149, 150, 151, 154, 160, 161, 162, 165, 169, 170, 172, 175, 180, 181, 182, 183, 186, 192, 194, 216,218
National Registration Act, 4
Newchurch Grammar School
NGS, 6, 1, 5, 7, 9, 10, 18, 19, 24, 74, 84, 86, 105, 134, 143, 153, 154, 158, 164, 165, 169, 203, 212
Nine Elms Cemetery, 161, 163
Nine Elms British Cemetery, 159, 163
Norfolk Regiment, 145, 174, 175, 176, 216
North Front Cemetery Gibraltar, 92, 95
North Lancashire Regiment, 45
Officer Long Number Papers, 34, 63, 169, 180
Ottoman Empire, 17
Outtersteene Communal Cemetery Extension, 104
Pals, 3, 14, 19, 34, 35, 169, 213, 214, 216
Passchendaele 77, 96, 98, 118, 120, 150, 215
Pickup, Rae 160
Pinnington, James 6, 181
Plymouth Naval Memorial, 51, 91
Poelcappelle, 107, 118, 119, 120, 150

219

Polygon Wood, 107
Poperinghe, 27, 83, 85, 113, 134, 137, 138, 157, 159, 161, 162, 163
Pozières British Cemetery, 147
Pozières Memorial, 143, 147, 148, 152
Prisoner of War Bureau, 182
Public School battalions, 14
Rawtenstall Cemetery, 199, 201, 202
Rawtenstall War Memorial, 16, 41, 95, 106, 195, 218
Ray, James 130
Register of Soldiers' Effects, 16, 27, 84, 85, 108, 117, 137, 188
Remy Siding, 137
Richebourg L'Avoue Military Cemetery, 12
Rifle Brigade, 34
Road Construction Company (RCC), 186, 209
Roclincourt Military Cemetery, 123, 128
Rossendale Free Press, 5, 9, 10, 13, 15, 18, 21, 25, 26, 38, 39, 48, 50, 51, 52, 68, 80, 81, 82, 93, 95, 114, 115, 116, 117, 138, 143, 146, 160, 163, 168, 169, 172, 173, 186, 187, 191, 192, 200, 217
Royal Army Medical Corps (RAMC), 144, 163, 205
Royal Engineers, 81, 118, 135, 159, 160, 161, 162, 186, 200, 209
Royal Field Artillery, 84, 160
West Lancashire Brigade, 85
Royal Flying Corps, 5, 47, 129, 131, 132
Royal Fusiliers, 14, 15, 20, 124, 125
Royal Garrison Artillery, 111, 165, 204
Royal Navy 47, 48, 49, 54, 55, 69, 88, 89, 90, 93, 94, 97
Royal Marine Light Infantry (RMLI), 52, 53, 68, 69, 70, 71, 216
Royal Scots, 155
Royal Warwickshire Regiment, 9, 10
Russia, 139, 196
Salient, 23, 85, 96, 102, 137, 171
Salonika, 192, 193
Shepherd, L Norman 88
'Shot at Dawn', 122
Slater, John 69
Smith, Henry (Harry) 187
Soldiers Died in the Great War, 15, 59, 200
Somme, 6, 4, 24, 28, 30, 32, 33, 34, 36, 39, 42, 43, 44, 56, 57, 58, 59, 65, 69, 77, 85, 102, 106, 112, 124, 140, 141, 143, 145, 147, 148, 151, 152, 170, 185, 213, 214, 215, 216
The Battle of, 11, 24, 32, 150, 215
South Wales Borderers, 10, 11, 216
Spanish Flu 196, 197, 198, 206
Stewart, Vernon 125
Stock, Reginald 203
Suvla Bay, 17, 19
Taylor, Arthur 112
Temperley, Jessie 119
The London Gazette, 19, 63
Thiepval, 33, 34, 35, 36, 42, 46, 58, 61

Thiepval Memorial to the Missing, 33, 36, 42
Thiepval Ridge, 34, 77, 82, 118
Titterington Albert, 106
Tomlinson, James 17
Training Reserve Batalion, 101, 106, 170, 180
Treaty of Brest-Litovsk, 139
Trickett's Memorial Ground, 152
Trones Wood, 45
Turnbull, J Percy 40
Tyne Cot, 29, 99, 105, 109, 116, 120, 213
Tyne Cot Cemetery, 29, 109, 213
Tyne Cot Memorial, 99
Verdun, 7, 24, 30, 77
Voormezeele Enc Cemetery 3 177
War Office, 21, 36, 69, 114, 132, 146, 147, 172, 182, 183, 187, 192, 194
West Yorkshire Regiment 25 ,26, 127, 216
Western Front, 6, 7, 22, 23, 24, 30, 65, 69, 77, 80, 88, 118, 148, 160, 166, 180, 189, 193, 197, 208, 214
Whittaker, Norman 164
Wilkinson, Norman 139
Winterbottom, John 96
Woodrow Wilson, President 87, 139
Wright, Edward 60
Yorkshire Post, 19, 21, 62, 217
Ypres, 3, 7, 11, 22, 23, 24, 27, 28, 77, 79, 85, 96, 97, 99, 102, 105, 106, 107, 108, 109, 110, 113, 114, 115, 120, 136, 137, 141, 142, 145, 150, 153, 157, 162, 171, 174, 178, 180, 213, 215, 218
First Battle of , 3, 4, 7
Second Battle of, 11, 96
Third Battle of, 74, 85, 96, 99, 108, 113, 115, 120, 150, 171, 215
Fourth Battle of, 141
Ypres Reservoir Cemetery, 110, 115
St George's Memorial Church, 213
Zonnebeke, 107, 116

Printed by Amazon Italia Logistica S.r.l.
Torrazza Piemonte (TO), Italy